The Order of the Sun and Moon, St Ives

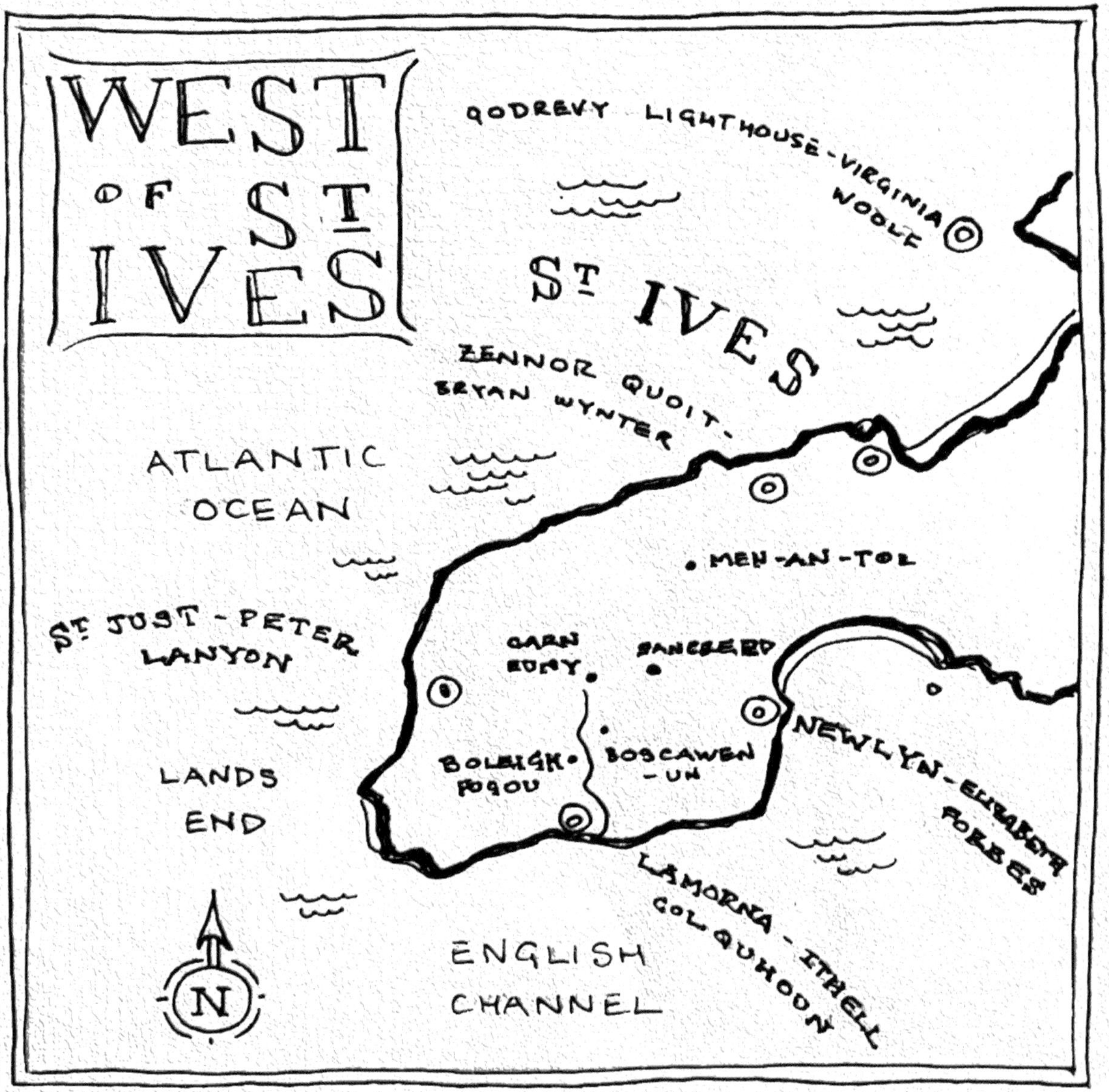
WEST OF ST IVES
GODREVY LIGHTHOUSE - VIRGINIA WOOLF
ST IVES
ZENNOR QUOIT - BRYAN WYNTER
ATLANTIC OCEAN
MEN-AN-TOL
ST JUST - PETER LANYON
CARN EUNY
SANCREED
BOLEIGH FOGOU
BOSCAWEN-UN
NEWLYN - ELIZABETH FORBES
LANDS END
LAMORNA - ITHELL COLQUHOUN
ENGLISH CHANNEL
N

The Order of the Sun and Moon, St Ives

Greg Humphries

Julian Vayne

Kate Southworth

The Universe Machine
Norwich
2023

First published 2023 by The Universe Machine, Norwich

ISBN 978-1-7398688-5-7

Contents

List of Illustrations

Preface

A beginning is a very delicate time.

The Order of the Sun and Moon, St Ives (OSM) will open an alchemical laboratory and ceremonial chamber in St Ives, Cornwall at The Crypt Gallery on the 4th of November 2023. This location will remain active as a node of transformative magic until the 9th of November.

In 1946, this art gallery saw the first breakaway exhibition by some of the modern abstract artists of the St Ives Society of Artists (STISA), who felt a strong need to set up their own distinct gallery. Appropriating the space directly beneath the church building which housed the mariners' chapel used as a gallery by the more traditionally minded STISA, the younger and more experimental artists in The Crypt Group held several exhibitions over the next few years, initially showing works by Peter Lanyon, Guido Morris, John Wells, Bryan Wynter, and Sven Berlin, who were subsequently joined by Barbara Hepworth, Ben Nicholson, Phil Whiting, Wilhelmina Barns-Graham, Guido Morris, Kit Baker, David Haughton, Adrian Ryan, and Patrick Heron amongst others. The Crypt Group soon developed into the Penwith Society of Arts in Cornwall, which also included many craftsmen amongst its membership, including the potter Bernard Leach who proposed the name.

The connection between landscape and abstract art celebrated by the artists of Cornwall fell out of fashion with the rise of Pop Art and more purist forms of abstractionism but has more recently become of great interest once again, and the St Ives artists recognised anew for their ground-breaking work.

Inside the container of this powerful psychogeography node, the OSM intend to continue this project further, showing ways that the abstract and the representational can converge, as the imaginal and rational likewise combine in the paradigms of occult artistic practice, where the reality of whether a thing portrays the mundane or the magical ultimately depends upon the stance of the viewer. It is this active participation of the viewer with the art, with the artist, which creates the esoteric and makes the work live, ensouling it in an animistic sense.

Nikki Wyrd
Norwich 2023

Acknowledgments

The Order of the Sun and Moon would like to thank:

Neil Scott, Emma Sharples and Amy Hale for their contribution to our online events, and for their enthusiastic support of the project. Judith Noble, for her Introduction to this volume and for her work in bringing the esoteric, the artistic and the academic worlds together. Nikki Wyrd for patiently and skilfully helping to edit, typeset and print this volume, for her marketing and design skills, and for her invaluable support. We would also like to express our gratitude to Treadwell's Books of London for hosting the online events, and supporting this project.
In acknowledgement of these vital contributions, The Order of the Sun and Moon, St Ives, are pleased to report that the Secret Chiefs have granted all those mentioned full membership of the Order.

Kate: I should like to acknowledge the radical work of art historian and cultural analyst Griselda Pollock, who, as one of my PhD supervisors many years ago, encouraged me to journey to the very edges of the thinkable. I offer gratitude to artist and psychoanalyst, Bracha Ettinger, about whose almost-unimaginable almost-theories I wrote my PhD. Her work continues to inspire and inform my approach to the world. I offer gratitude to soul mates who speak the green language, touch the unseen and find ways to share this with others. Especially I offer my deepest gratitude and love to artist, photographer, filmmaker, Graham Gaunt, with whom I encounter the magic and mysteries of the moors, stars and birds.

Greg: I would like to acknowledge the contribution of all the occult artists recognised and unrecognised on whose mighty shoulders we stand, principally Ithell Colquhoun without whom this exhibition would never have happened. On a personal note I would like to thank Daro Montag and the contributors to the RANE research cluster at Falmouth University for expanding my vision of what an art practice could be; and all the members of the magical organisations I have been a member of over the years (OBOD , TOPY, IOT and the Church Of Santo Daime) who opened the doorways to a vision of what an expanded world could be.

I would also recognise the non-human and other dimensional beings who guide and protect the work in this world and all the others (you know who you are) and finally Francesca, Eleanor and Robyn who put up with all these shenanigans.

Julian: I would like to acknowledge Ronald Hutton who, over twenty years ago, suggested that Greg Humphries and I might like to meet. I am also grateful to Elizabeth Tomos and Cavan McLaughlin for inviting me to exhibit my work in 2022 at the Trans-States conference. I would like to personally thank Nikki Wyrd, the most excellent editor, publisher, magician, friend, teacher, companion and much more, and offer you my love and deepest respect. I offer my gratitude to the lineage of magical practitioners, and wish blessings on those to come after us. From the heights of the heavens, to the depths of the earth. We are one heart. Connected.

Introduction

The Order of the Sun and Moon are three artists (Greg Humphries, Kate Southworth and Julian Vayne) working within a magical context who have drawn inspiration from the work of Ithell Colquhoun, so it is fitting that the first public manifestation of the Order's work should take place in St Ives, close to Lamorna in West Cornwall where Colquhoun worked for many years, and a town where she enjoyed friendships with fellow artists. For Colquhoun, art and the magical, the occult and the esoteric were not separate practices, but one indivisible whole. Making art was for her an act of magic, and this approach meant that her work was frequently overlooked by the predominantly materialist art world during her lifetime. For a quarter of a century after her death in 1988, Colquhoun's work languished (literally, in a damp outbuilding), ignored by the art world and hidden from public view. During this time, it was the occult community in Cornwall that kept her memory alive and championed her work. This, coupled with an insistence by mainly feminist scholars that the work of the women artists associated with Surrealism, including Colquhoun, should be properly studied and critiqued, has led to a new-found recognition and respect. Colquhoun is now recognised as one of Britain's leading 20th century artists and the first major retrospective of her work will take place at Tate St Ives in 2024.

Colquhoun and fellow Surrealists including Leonora Carrington, Remedios Varo, Leonor Fini and Meret Oppenheim used Surrealist creative techniques to delve into their own psyches, and the occult took centre stage in their work in a variety of very personal ways. Many of these techniques, which Colquhoun continued to use throughout her long career, are in themselves highly effective and transformational methods of working magic. Filmmaker Maya Deren, much of whose work was made in dialogue with the Surrealists in the 1940s, described herself as an artist-magician whose task was not only to explore the inner worlds of magic and vision, but also to make those worlds visible to others through her work. In recent years, artists including those who make up the Order of the Sun and Moon, have understood this task and have begun to explore the magical and occult in many ways and with a growing confidence.

Colquhoun's practice was fundamentally inspired by the ensouled landscapes of Cornwall; its 'Living Stones'[1]. These places were the well-spring of much of her work, which in its turn has provided a rich and compelling map to guide the Initiates of the Order of the Sun and Moon on their own inner world voyages. The land itself, with its spirits and its more than human inhabitants, insists that artists should listen to it and make work that respects and honours it. The artist-magicians of the Order of the Sun and Moon have listened to the land of Cornwall and its spirits, and are part of Colquhoun's lineage. Their work demonstrates that the art is the magic and that the magic is the art.

Judith Noble
Professor of Film and the Occult (arts University Plymouth) and editor, *The Dance of Moon and Sun – Ithell Colquhoun, British Women and Surrealism.*

---

[1] See Ithell Colquhoun, *The Living Stones: Cornwall* (1957, Peter Owen)

The Order of the Sun and Moon: Art and the Occult in the 21st Century

Greg Humphries

'Occult: of or relating to magic, alchemy, astrology, theosophy, or other practical arts held to involve agencies of a secret or mysterious nature.' OED

'Magic is the process by which the tools and techniques of the imagination can be used to affect consensus reality.' Julian Vayne.

The title of this publication, and the exhibition it relates to, 'The Order of the Sun and Moon, St Ives' (OSM) is an idea that arises from an essay, 'The Order of the Sun and Moon, Nicaragua', written by artist and occultist Ithell Colquhoun after a dream she had in the 1940s, whilst she was living no more than 20 miles from where I write this in Cornwall. In it she relates a dream she had of a magical order of individuals and the 'grotto' in which they practised their magical art. She explains that the Nicaragua referred to should not be thought of geographically, but rather as an exotic 'other' place (similar to the concept of India in early alchemical texts) which is not real in our plane of existence. Similarly, my hope for this exhibition is that for a temporary period of time we can instigate OSM as a crucible in which we can open the audience to otherworldly agency, the possibility for something incredible to be manifest in this world. As Colquhoun states in her essay: 'For some reason I obtained a glimpse of this mysterious centre, and now if I receive an idea or perception which does not seem to be a direct result of anything I have read, heard or thought, I take it to be a message from the order'.

Moving towards a 21st Century definition of Occult, or Esoteric, Art.

This is a shifting, slippery and tricky thing to define and its meaning has changed, and continues to change, depending on temporal and cultural phenomena. However, a good starting point for a 21st century definition of occult/esoteric art is outlined by the thinker Marco Pasi in his essay 'Coming Forth By Night' where he outlines four contexts in which esoteric art is created:

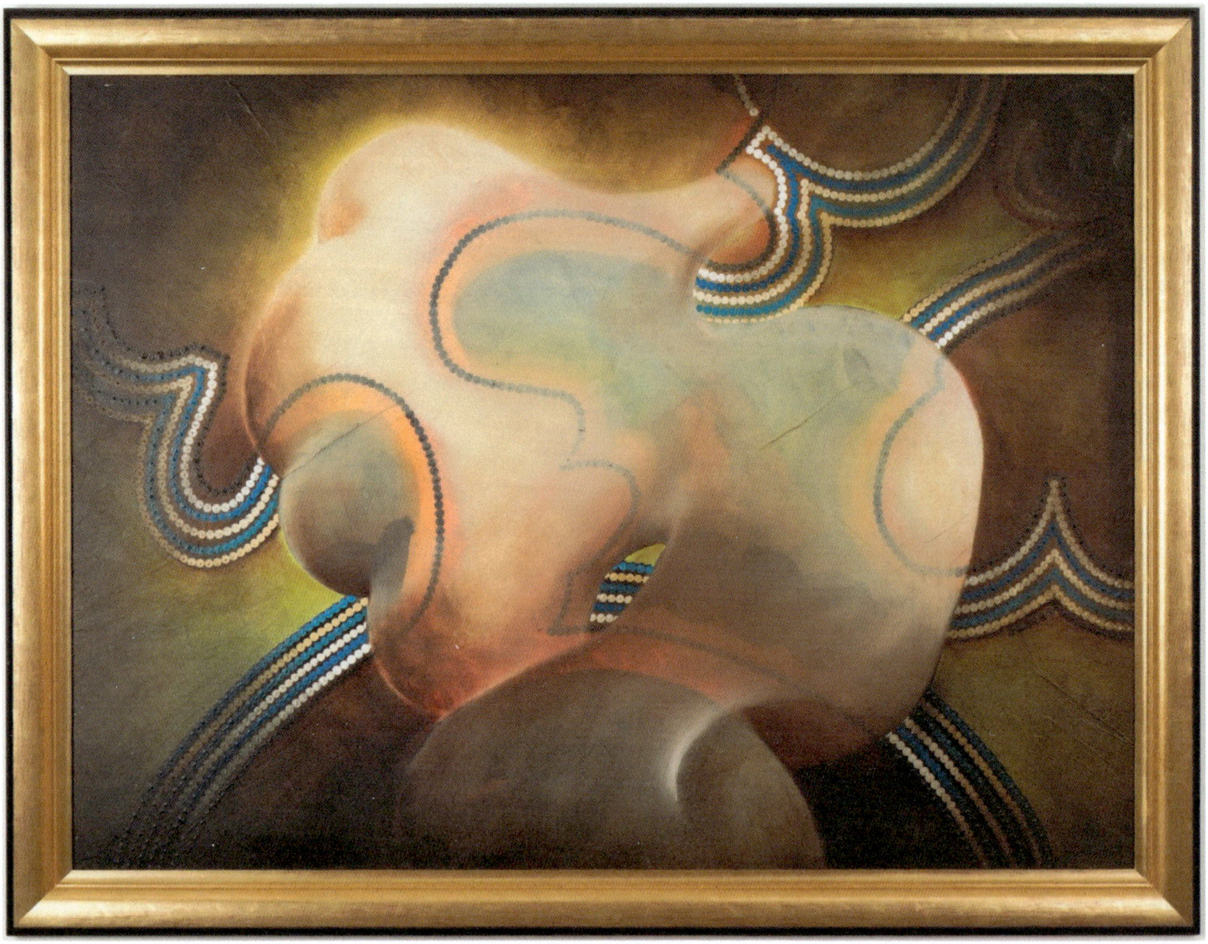

Figure 1 'Lost and Found: The Anaconda Brings Its Gifts', 2023

- The representation of esoteric symbols or images.
- The production of an esoteric object that can be treated as a fetishistic item.
- The work is produced to induce a spiritual or extraordinary experience.
- The work is created as a result of contact with spiritual entities.

In addition I believe an occult (or esoteric) philosophy incorporates a belief in objective 'Otherworlds', or dimensions. The language we use here is important because although, it could be argued, that Freud et al are describing the same otherworldly phenomena, psycho-analytical/scientific thinking describes such experiences as arising from within the individual's subconscious mind; but that does not really convey the experience it attempts to describe. It abstracts the occult experience of Otherworlds and detaches the 'experiencer' from the experience. I don't believe this is useful or desirable for the Esoteric artist as it is precisely this experience they are trying to communicate to an audience.

One charge which has often been levelled at Esoteric Artists is that they must be unhinged mentally to believe in objective Otherworlds. In answer I would quote the occult/surrealist painter Leonora Carrington who said that when people queried whether Otherworlds really existed, she would simply reply 'Do you not dream?'.

Apart from the World of Dreams, more examples of 'Other', alternative, but objective worlds are:

The place where ideas come from and exist. This is described by Alan Moore as the 'ideasphere'.

The place people 'go to' when they die. Traditionally this has been described as the Place of the Dead or 'Ancestors'.

Now, there are innumerable ways to conceptualise and describe these worlds, but I would argue that we can all agree they exist, even though they are 'hidden' and not accessible to our everyday consciousness. However, through the tools and techniques of the imagination (i.e. magic) we can access them, interact and be in very real relation to the entities we find there.

Interestingly, I recently had a conversation about this with someone who understood these tools and techniques (and by extension magic itself) to be inherently evil, as they were 'used by mass media to control people'. Whether we believe that statement is true or not it highlights a viewpoint that has echoed throughout history from the witch trials of the 16–17th century to the fabricated 'Satanic Child Abuse' accusations of the 1990s. Obviously, I don't subscribe to this view. In my opinion magic is a neutral force, technology, or spirit, that can be collaborated with on any goal determined by the Will of the magician. Magic itself does not have an ethical standpoint, rather it is the ethics of the user that determine the flavour of the outcome.

Why now? There is currently a re-assessment of the influence of esoteric/occult philosophy and the arts, in particular the influence of Women Artists and occultists on Surrealism and Abstract art; for example, summer 2022 in Venice saw both the Peggy Gugenheim Collection exhibition *Surrealism and Magic: Enchanted Modernity*,[i] and the Venice Biennale's main exhibition *The Milk of Dreams*[ii]. Many beliefs that have traditionally been repressed and marginalised are being re-examined and brought into the light. In this sense, the occult is becoming a part of mainstream culture.

In writing this essay, organising this exhibition, and reviving the concept of OSM, I wanted to join in this conversation regarding the increasing cultural acceptance of magical, esoteric and occult philosophy which seems to go hand in hand with a re-assessment and acceptance of feminist and queer viewpoints. Occult practitioners have been marginalised for hundreds of years, forcing them to hide their activities and work, often under the threat of torture and death from the prevailing culture. In the West this resurgence and acceptance of Occult art and its practitioners is very new and, to be honest, I don't know how long it will last. One driving force for OSM is to grab this possibly small window of opportunity to get our voices heard before mainstream culture starts to build the bonfires and chant 'Burn The Witch!!' again. Whilst the esoteric is flavour of the decade at present, the artists in this exhibition are fully aware that coming out of the 'occult closet' in this way is not without risk, both professionally and physically, and by sticking our heads above the parapet we are placing ourselves in the cultural sniper's sights.

For me, my work is concerned with climate crisis and (re)connecting people to Nature as a way of mitigating the effects of pollution, ecocide and rising global temperatures. I see these as a consequence of us 'othering' Nature and cutting ourselves off emotionally from the harm we cause to the biosphere. If we can re-connect with Nature the harm we cause would be felt emotionally and we simply would not do it Outwardly my work looks like a journey of land art, outdoor education, painting and sculpture; but inwardly this has also been a personal journey deepening my own relationship with the natural world which involves animism and acceptance of a magical realist philosophy.

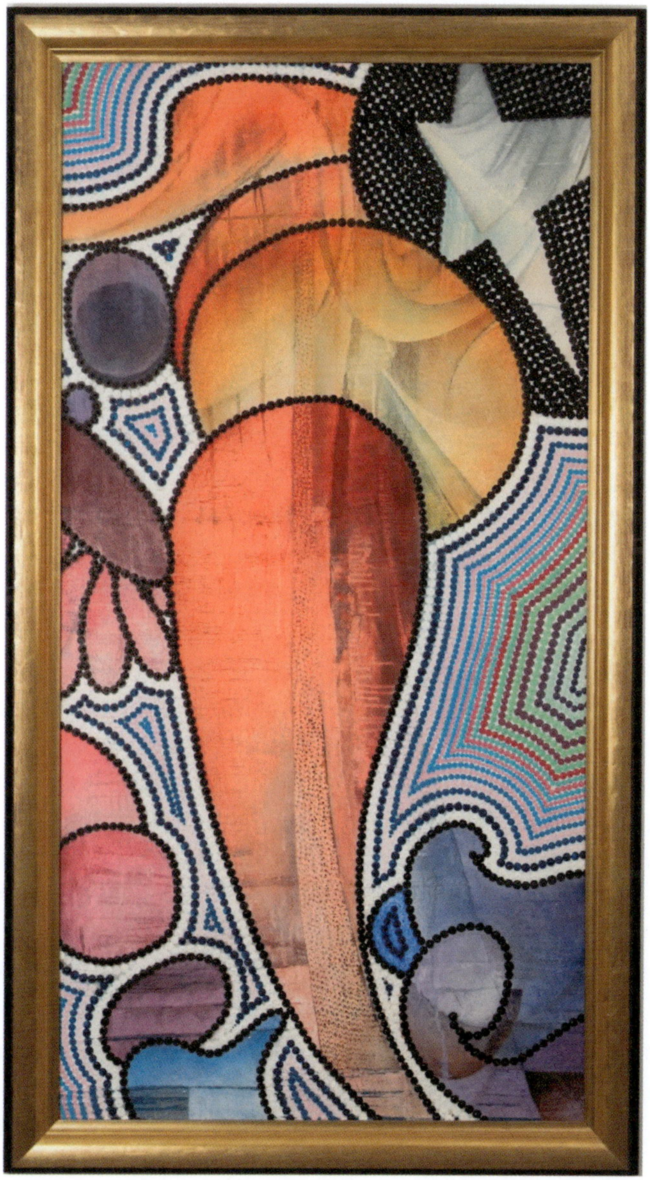

Figure 2 'Charon Ferries Orpheus Across The River - Aust Ferry, 12th May 1966', 2011

From early teenage years I've known something was amiss. Some split, or schism had taken place that meant we were all separated from Nature, the Ancestors, our Dreams and the Gods.

I remember wandering with friends in Clipstone Woods near our school during lunchbreaks; moving away from the coalmine and council estate to a green wonderland full of mystery and beings that were just out of reach. I would construct stories in my head, of imaginary encounters with the gladiators that fought again and again in the colosseum of the abandoned sewage works; or the cloaked and shrouded elves that ran among the trees of the deepest parts of the remnants of Sherwood Forest.

In this way I can see myself trying to find ways to mend the split between the worlds, using story and imagination. A grounding which was untamed and was to stand me in good stead when I deepened my explorations of bringing the worlds together through magical practice and the Western Mystery Tradition. First the Order of Bards, Ovates and Druids which gave me an existing mythology, a structure and a framework in which to place and understand my experiences; and then Chaos Magic which gave me the freedom to find a system that worked for myself.

But why magic and animism? Why hark back to a mindset that has long been proven by science to be false, hubris, useless and defunct? Maybe because in the context of the current ecological and climate crisis we are understanding that science does not have all the answers, particularly when it is faced with economic and political realities. We can't see a way through this crisis to a bright, optimistic, and beautiful future.

What brought this into stark contrast for me was a realisation I had during an online course I recently ran in psychogeography and landscape art. During the course the twelve students and myself examined a location as a case study: exploring what the location was used for (and who had owned it) in the past, and how that affected the place in the present. All this was fine, until I asked the students to project into the future what the place could be used for and who would own it. I invited them to get as 'science fiction' as they liked and imagine both a dystopian option and a utopian option for that place. The students were able to imagine any number of horrific, terrifying and apocalyptic scenarios for this poor little piece of land; yet not one of them could conceive of what a utopian future may even possibly look like. Not one.

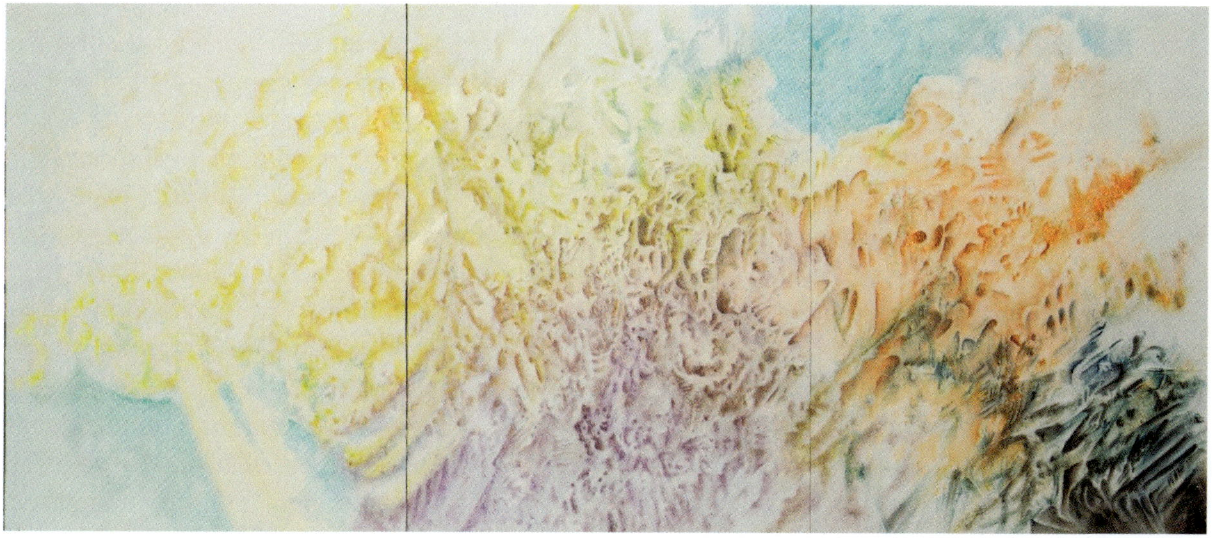

Figure 3 'Inspiration Descends On The Breeze From Mercury's Heels: From Kether To Malkuth', 2023

This small example made me realise this is generally where we are on a macro scale when considering ecological collapse and climate change. We can't (and I include myself in this) even imagine a way through to a bright, optimistic, beautiful, and balanced world; and this is a problem if we understand the imagination to be the first step towards manifestation.

Nothing was ever created in this world without it being imagined first, and creativity is just that—an act of creation. As humans we have the ability to imagine something (or have an idea) and make it real in this world as an object, painting, sculpture, business, performance or whatever. And as artists (and magicians) we work with the tools and techniques of the imagination on a daily basis; so what can we do to help? Surely, if anyone has the ability to imagine a better future than the current apocalyptic 'end of days' that is the morass we find ourselves in, it is our duty to do so. I would even take that thought a step further and argue that it is our responsibility, as artists and magicians, to use the magical tools and techniques we have to imagine our way out of this mess. Who else has more tools to do it than us?

From my own personal experience, I understand how difficult this is. There seems to be a creative block when I try and go there. Trying to imagine an idyllic future is impossible because we see only the reality we are conditioned to see by our culture, memories, geography, family history etc. These influences necessarily colour our view of the world. The Situationists understood this and so did Timothy Leary who described our experience of the world as if we see reality from the inside of our own personal 'Reality Tunnel', constructed from all of these prior beliefs.

From inside my own 'Reality Tunnel', how is it possible to see beyond its limitations towards something bigger and better?

I'm not sure this is possible, and certainly not working alone, so in the context of this exhibition and the setting up of OSM I want to propose a different way of looking at this...

The times are changing. The author John Higgs writes of the 20th century as being a period of increasing individualisation leading to the Postmodern concept that all truths are relative, where all that matters is that truth which I say is correct. This can be seen manifest in the apparently consequence-less 'Every Man for Himself' political and cultural philosophy of the 1980s. It can also be seen in the myth of the lone suffering artist, struggling alone in a studio to create a new art object, emerging into the world to present the work that they alone have created.

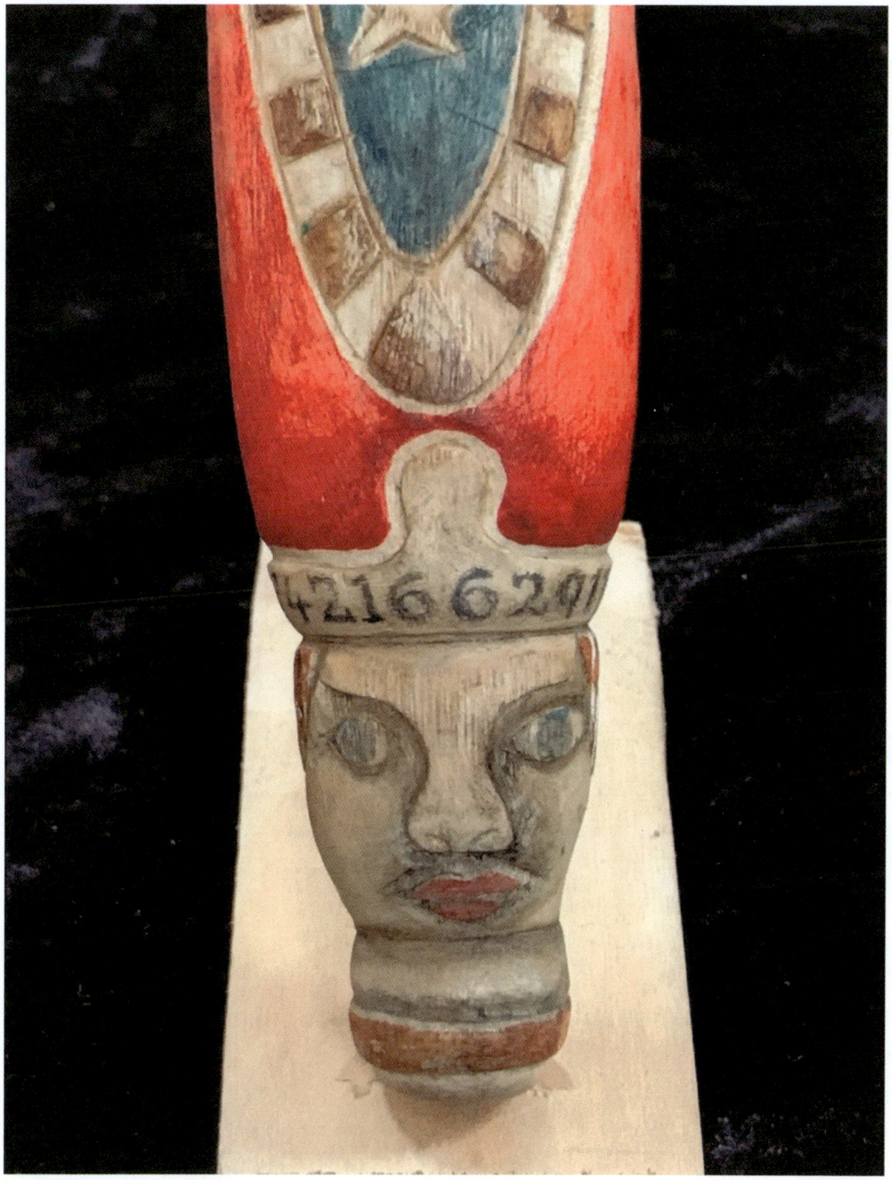

Figure 4 'The Princess Keeps Open The Doors of Perception', 2016

With the dawn of the 21st century, and the emergence of Generation Z (those born between 1990 and 2010), there is an understanding that whilst we are indeed all individuals, with increased access to portable internet-based technology we are all very much connected. The actions we perform are not without consequences and others are profoundly affected by what we do. With this realisation it may be better to approach the Climate Crisis as a collective. A group of individuals working in collaboration towards a goal rather than in competition with each other, in a spirit of cooperation.

'*Animism: The attribution of a living soul to plants, inanimate objects, and natural phenomena.*' OED

Animism presents the possibility of not excluding (or 'othering') the Natural World in this process. If we see everything around us through this lens, then everything has a soul or spirit; and rather than seeing those things as separate from us it places us in relationship with them, which then allows the possibility to enter into a relationship with the Natural World on a level that is mutually respectful. Working together towards the mutually beneficial goal of a positive future beyond Climate Crisis is surely better than us humans trying to do it alone.

Creating works of art that collaboratively attempt to communicate the messages of Otherworldly beings (be that the Ancestral World, Natural World, Dream World or any Other World) in order to help us at this time, might be one way to approach a 21st century Occult/Art practice. As occultists we can conceive of opening a portal to another world and starting communication with the beings there to help us with the current ecological, climate crisis.

In her work, the esoteric artist Ithell Colquhoun explored the idea that colour could open new ways of seeing, and being, in a viewer. It was something Colquhoun used in her work throughout her life, culminating in *Taro As Colour* (1977) which provides a completely abstract, colour-only Tarot pack designed to be a portal to 'other worlds' and to open other planes of reality to the viewer if meditated upon. For *Taro* she utilised the colour scheme developed by the occult magical group called the 'Hermetic Order of the Golden Dawn' (HOGD) which developed an initiatory system that combined colour theory with the Kabbalah, astrology, numerology, and various consciousness altering techniques to attain a path to enlightenment.

Colquhoun was particularly interested in how colour could affect the viewer, both physically and psychically. She sought to join the Hermetic Order of The Golden Dawn in the 1930s, but was unsuccessful. It is easy to see why this group was enticing for Colquhoun. The HOGD system of magic treats colours themselves as entities that could be invoked, and these colours represent energetic signatures of forces that act on this world. When combined with a disciplined, prolonged study of the attributes and correspondences of each colour, a new way of seeing the world is developed in the initiate. The attributes of the colours used were linked to the pathways of the Kabbalistic Tree of Life, astrology, and the tarot.For example, Colquhoun's *Taro* card 'The Children of The Voice: the Oracles of The Mighty Gods', depicts three roughly concentric circles of colour against a reddish grey-inclining to mauve background. The descending inner circle is orange, which is surrounded by, and blends with pale mauve, and that in turn is surrounded by new-leather yellow.

If the HOGD system is followed we would understand this card is also The Lovers in the traditional Tarot. With a key scale of numerical value 17, the four colours correspond with the Four Scales of Colour:

- The Knight::Orange
- The Queen::Pale Mauve
- The Prince::New Leather Yellow
- The Princess::Reddish Grey/inclined to Mauve

In the Kabbalah these describe different aspects of the Path from Binah::The Great Mother to Tiphareth::The Heart. In the HOGD system these aspects need to be learned and understood for each card. There are also astrological and numerical attributes to be learned for each, in order to help describe through metaphor the qualities of the card.

However, in her *Taro*, Colquhoun is offering us something different. Each card is presented as a focus for meditation. Through this type of repeated familiarisation over an extended period of time, the spirits of the colours themselves are activated and can be communicated with. Each card acts as a portal to a particular other world.

There was an understanding of abstract Colour Theory in the system, particularly the use of Simultaneous Contrast, as espoused by Kandinsky, Mondrian and other abstract artists of the 20th century. We are starting to understand this arises from ideas within the occult & magical Theosophist movement who attributed colours to various psychic phenomena (auras etc). It is said Colquhoun learned 'Colour Theory' from the modernist Architect Amedee Ozenfant (who founded the Purist movement with Le Corbusier) whose atelier she worked in during 1936.

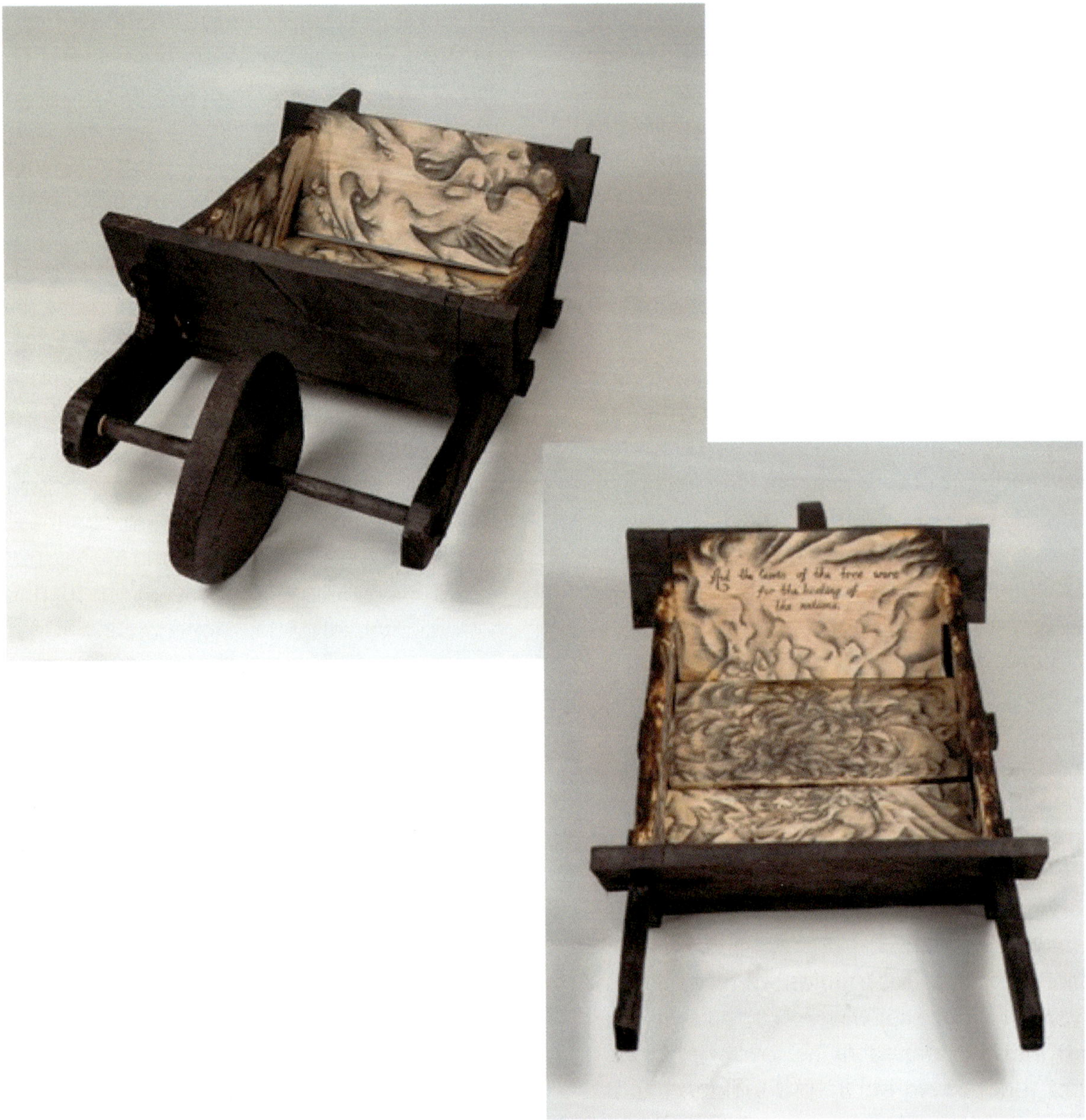

Figure 5 'From The Ash Will Arise New Hope', 2023

Colour also acts as an essential element in the work I produce. I use simultaneous Contrast and the HOGD Scales of Colour extensively, as a way to attempt to induce an extraordinary experience in the viewer, and the HOGD system provides a framework of attributes for the occult scholar to gain deeper insight into the experience they are having.

I collaboratively help create artworks which act as objects that I describe as arising from a 'Future Archaeology'. That is, they have arisen from contacting entities that exist in a 4- or 5-dimensional space, as enigmatic objects to behave as clues to potential New Worlds for the viewer. They are not intended as visions of New Worlds for the viewer to passively inhabit, but as potential portals for us all to enter and envision our own futures, beyond the Climate Apocalypse that currently threatens us.

As an example, for my piece 'From The Ash Will Arise New Hope', 2023 I wanted to create a symbol of Hope for a new future beyond the Climate Crisis we are facing. I wanted to make this work collaboratively with other people, and also the Spirits of Nature. So, as part of a residency at Kestle Barton, Cornwall I invited people to help me construct a mediaeval wheelbarrow, from an ash tree felled locally due to Ash Dieback disease, and decorate it with abstract/automatic imagery gathered from sitting in silence at Kestle Barton's wildflower meadow.

There are many apocalyptic narratives around Climate Change, and I would like to explore and question these. As artists and occultists we have the power of creation, the ability to have ideas, thoughts and images in our heads that we can make manifest in Consensus Reality; outside of ourselves.

These manifestations may appear as artworks, architecture, objects, communities, businesses etc. and through this process we co-create the world around us. I believe it is our duty, and responsibility, to create a world that humanity, our children, and their children in turn, will thrive in.

The idea of an apocalypse, or 'the end of days', has recurred throughout history and generally this has been seen in terms of an extinction event for humanity; everybody dies. However, despite some serious calamities, humanity has always recovered, and these events (although terrible, traumatic and involving the death of many people) always precipitated a change in the established order of things. In this way I see Death as a transformation process as opposed to a final one. For example, the Black Death in the mid-14th century precipitated the end of the feudal system due to labour shortages. It saw the rise of the wheelbarrow as an acceptable and desirable tool. As such, the wheelbarrow is a symbol of hope. A symbol to remind us that we will survive as a species beyond the current impending Climate disaster and Ecocide, and that after this Death, new life will arise.

In Northern European mythology the tree that connects all the worlds is an ash tree. When it dies it is said it will be 'the end of time'; Ragnarok. *Hymenoscyphus fraxineus* is a spore borne fungal disease that is currently ravaging the UK and western Europe. Current predictions are that 95% of the ash trees will die, much to the great sorrow of those who love them, and who hold individual trees dear to their hearts. However, a few will survive, and these trees could be used to re-stock and re-build a genetically stronger ash population. In itself the ash tree is a poignant metaphor for humanity's current situation and I wanted to highlight that there is hope beyond this incredibly painful, desperate and seemingly overwhelming situation.

The meadow at Kestle is a place that only exists due to human intervention. The yearly cutting of the meadow and removal of material creates a nutrient deficient soil, which allows the flowers to grow the following year. Without this yearly apocalypse bracken, bramble and scrub would dominate the area, reducing the biodiversity, flora and fauna. In this way death is a necessary precursor to more complex new life; what can seem destructive, catastrophic and 'the end of days' in September brings the hope of flowers in the Spring.

On an occult level, sitting in meditative silence can allow the spirits of that place to whisper in your ear or guide your hand as it moves across a page. In this way the spirits of the Nature can use the artist's body as a channel through which they can communicate with a wider audience. This is an opportunity to be part of a truly collaborative process with non-human entities and brings into question the idea of the artist as sole creator of an artwork.

On a practical level I want to equip the audience with some practical skills and knowledge that may be useful to them in this—or some post-Climate Crisis—world, however bad that could get. Coincidentally the same skills also lead the practitioner to a more sustainable current lifestyle. Leading them through the process of making a wheelbarrow from first principles using only edged tools and locally sourced trees seemed a good way to address this. It is not that I expect people to immediately go out and make their own wooden wheelbarrows, rather that they could have the knowledge and ability to do so if they ever found the need, as well as overcoming the fear of attempting other similar tasks.

My way of understanding Occult Art in the 21st century is for the art to be in service to an ongoing esoteric practice, and for the artist to act as a channel to create artwork that engages with the challenges of the times we live in. I am not interested in presenting a vision of a Utopian future reality. Rather I am interested in presenting work that gives the opportunity for the viewer to move towards a greater understanding and engagement with the Otherworlds we encounter, including the Natural World, and through this connection we can work together at creating a new vision for all our futures.

---

[i] Surrealism and Magic: Enchanted Modernity was a joint exhibition project between the Peggy Guggenheim Collection and the Museum Barberini. https://www.guggenheim-venice.it/en/whats-on/exhibitions/surrealism-and-magic-enchanted-modernity/

[ii] La Biennale di Venezia, statement by Cecilia Alemani. https://www.labiennale.org/en/art/2022/statement-cecilia-alemani

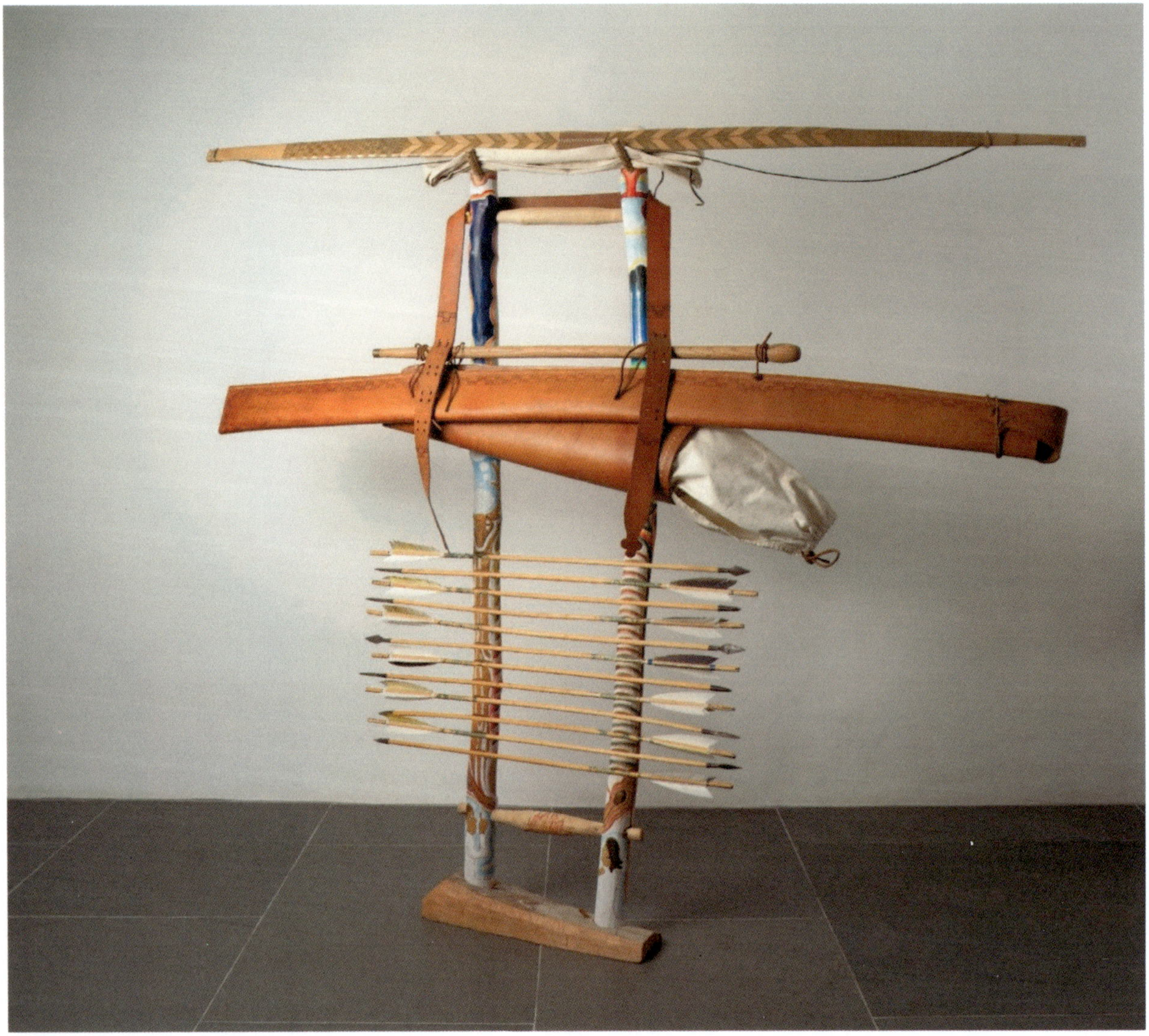

Figure 6 'For The Herald Of The New Aeon', 2019

Reading List

Ithell Colquhoun: *Taro As Colour*, Fulgur, London, 2018.

Aleister Crowley (Master Therion): *The Book of Thoth: A Short Essay on the Tarot of The Egyptians*, Samuel Weiser Inc., New York, 1974.

Johannes Itten: 'Kunst De Farbe', Studienausgabe, 1944.

Richard Shillitoe (ed.): *Medea's Charms: Selected Shorter Writing of Ithell Colquhoun*, Peter Owen Publishers, London, 2019.

'Communist Witches and Cyborg Magic: The Emergence of Queer, Feminist, Esoteric Futurism'. Essay by Amy Hale for Burlington Contemporary, 2022.

Marco Pasi: 'Coming Forth By Night', in A. Valliant (ed): *Options With Nostrils*, Berlin, 2010, pp103–11.

The Art of Magic & the Magic of Art

Julian Vayne

There is a black world, criss-crossed by vivid lines of light. Impossibly fine filaments stretching towards vanishing points light-years distant. There are arcane, wriggling characters and concentric circles, undulating ripples expanding outward into an inky-black void. This monochrome wonderland is simultaneously a vast volume of interstellar space, and a subterranean cavernous of vertiginous dimensions. The measureless chasm in which these visions appear is also no greater than the distance between my eyes and the ceiling, which now comes into focus. The blackness becomes white, the white lines invert into the dark crevasses between the tiles of the hospital ceiling. My depth perception begins to return, though my left eye is covered with dressing that will not be removed for several days. I am in hospital, aged five, and the surgeons have corrected the squint I was born with. The anaesthesia is wearing off but the experience of this re-emergence into awareness, with its attendant sense of strangeness, profound familiarity and out-of-body perception will stay with me for years to come. Many years later, I would snort a fat line of grey powder in Goa and remember that first infantile psychedelic experience. Ketamine, first synthesized in 1962, was rapidly adopted as the anaesthetic of choice for children, burns victims, the elderly, and horses. For decades this weird molecule was believed to only exist as the synthetic creation of humans until a paper published in 2020 identified it as the poison produced by the nematophagous fungus *Pochonia chlamydospori.* This chemical portal to what Marcia Moore, the High Priestess of ketamine, described as 'the bright world', was the first exogenously induced altered state I encountered. It would not be the last.

The relationship between art and magic is a close one, with magic itself commonly referred to as both an art and science. Many magicians are artists in one way or another. The ritual events, the ceremonies that we curate, are themselves a form of installation or performance art.

The very idea of The Great Work, the sculpting of the self through esoteric practice, shades off into the 'magnum opus' or 'oeuvre' of the artist. The physical or performative art of magic leaves tangible traces of spiritual transformation in much the same way that the gold of alchemy is the material expression of inner practice.

Magical art may be expressed in poetry, music, dance, the blended perfumes of incense or many other forms, and often includes the crafting of physical art objects. Magical art may manifest as ritual chambers with elaborate altars dedicated to particular spirits, or marks on the floor, drawn with flour or marked out with masking tape, indicating the delineation of zones of power. Magical art may be temporary graphical pieces; short-lived sigilised intentions, drawn on paper, destined for Fluxus style immolation, or more permanent creations such as the tattooing of skin, or the carving of stone.[i]

One example of such an installation, from a decade or so ago, was a ritual I curated which featured the spirit beings initially conjured into existence by American actor, animator, filmmaker, and musician Mike Judge. These entities, known as Beavis and Butt-Head, are depicted as slacker adolescents. They represent the qualities of apathy, low-brow humour, sexism, stunted intelligence, and cruelty. The purpose of the ritual—which took place in a venue beneath the railway arches at the grotty end of Bethnal Green—was an evocation and a binding of these spirits. Beavis and Butt-Head were taken to represent the trash MTV, tabloid culture that glories in stupidity and hates anything that it can't understand. Specifically, the intention of the rite was to challenge anti-intellectualism, particularly among working class British cultures. I grew up in such a working class setting and as a reasonably clever kid found out early on that being bespectacled (see the eye operation mentioned above) and a reader (nicknamed 'Brains' while I was still in Infant School) was not by any means a cause for celebration. At times both within my family and my wider culture there was an uneasy relationship between the display of knowledge and the ability to belong. To be considered clever was to be marked out as different, and deviation from the established proletariat norms was punishable by anything from derisory comments through to social exclusion or, if you were really unlucky, a good kicking.

The process behind the Beavis and Butt-Head ritual was one I've used several times, in part inspired by my study of the Japanese martial art Aikido. In Aikido one of the aims of the practice is to blend oneself with the mechanical and subtle emotional process of an aggressor. This blending allows the practitioner to rapidly develop a felt sense of the attacker, to know where and how they are likely to move. To in sense become them, thus enabling the Aikido practitioner to find just the right moment and location to make a

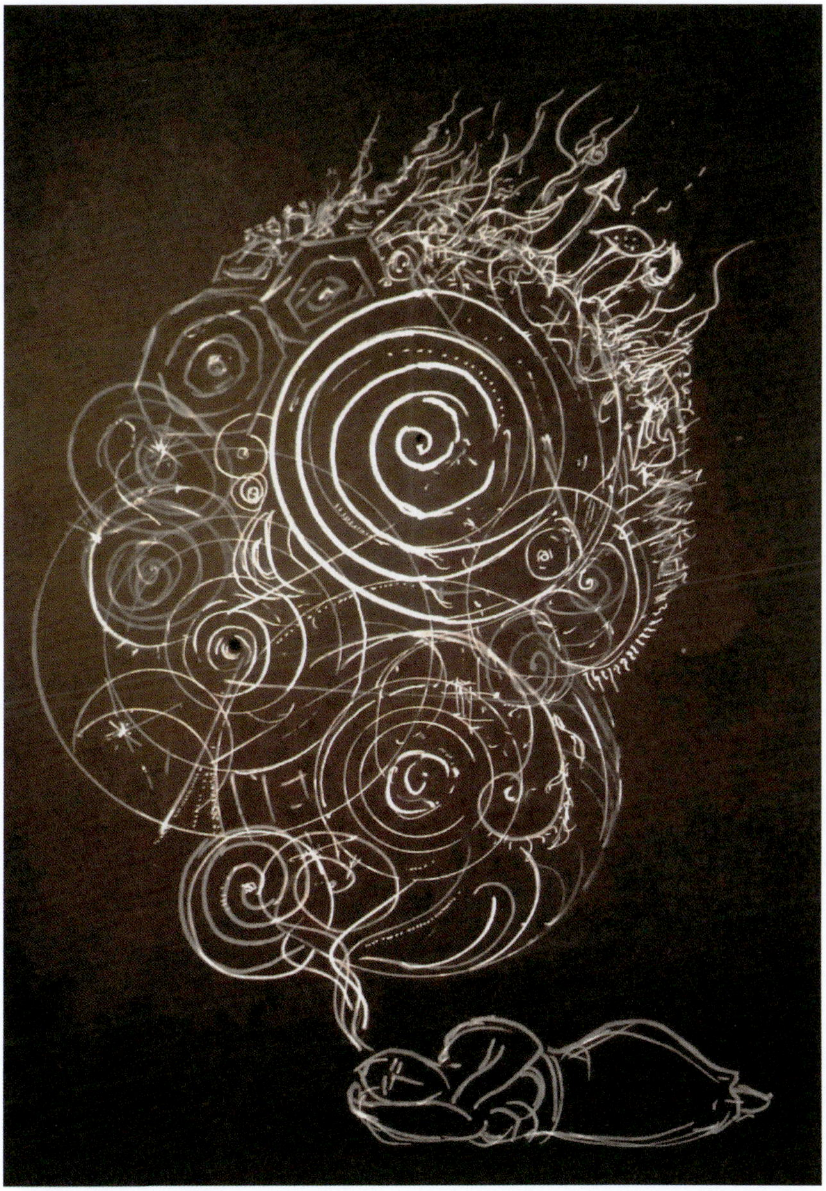

Figure 7 'Underworld Dreaming', 2022

defensive move, and to redirect the impetus of the aggressor against themselves. By blending with the person we are fighting, we discover the best way to end the conflict.

To do this with the anti-intellectualism represented by Beavis and Butt-Head, video clips of these characters were projected on the ceiling and walls of the chamber using multiple data projectors. The curved walls of the chamber became the canvas upon which these caricatures of banal youth-culture grinned and gurned. Speakers in the temple blared their mindless mantra 'da, da, dah-dah-dah, da da, dah-dah-dah...' Participants in the ritual circumambulated around two members of the group who were seated in the centre of the temple. The circling magicians, stamping an arrhythmic round, intoned the gormless song and summoned their own feelings of anti-intellectualism; all those times they had been harmed by it, all those times they had been responsible for it, all those times they had been complicit with it. They blended their minds with the jeering figures of Beavis and Butt-Head; but the full incorporation of these spirits was undertaken by the two practitioners seated in the centre of the circle. While the others whirled about these two magicians, who would connect most deeply with the Beavis and Butt-Head force, were eating. Earlier that day we had purchased a bewildering range of highly coloured sweets and fizzy drinks. Now as the whole group descended into the vacuous mindspace the couple in the centre of the circle gorged themselves on improbable blue-coloured soda and ripped into packets of gummy sweets. Highly coloured candies and synthetic-tasting confectionery were wolfed down with vast quantities of diabetes-inducing sugary drinks. Collectively, as the blaring music played and the 'da, da dah-dah-dah' mantra reached a crescendo, we descended into the place of the intentionally stupid, the glorification of idiocracy, and the hatred of anything that dared to step out of line, to be curious, or to wish for something more than TV dinners and celebrity culture.

Once we had blended Aikido style with this force, and our brave operators in the centre had consumed a prodigious quality of ghastly confectionery, we switched gears. The images in the chamber were replaced with a panoply of artworks drawn from a bewildering variety of cultures, the sound of Johann Sebastian Bach replacing the mindless mantra and, selecting slips of paper at random from a hat, those circling around the sugar-intoxicated duo in the centre of the temple, read aloud erudite quotes from philosophers, poets, scientists and others. This functioned as a banishing ritual. The couple in the centre who embodied the spirits of Beavis and Butt-head began to gag and

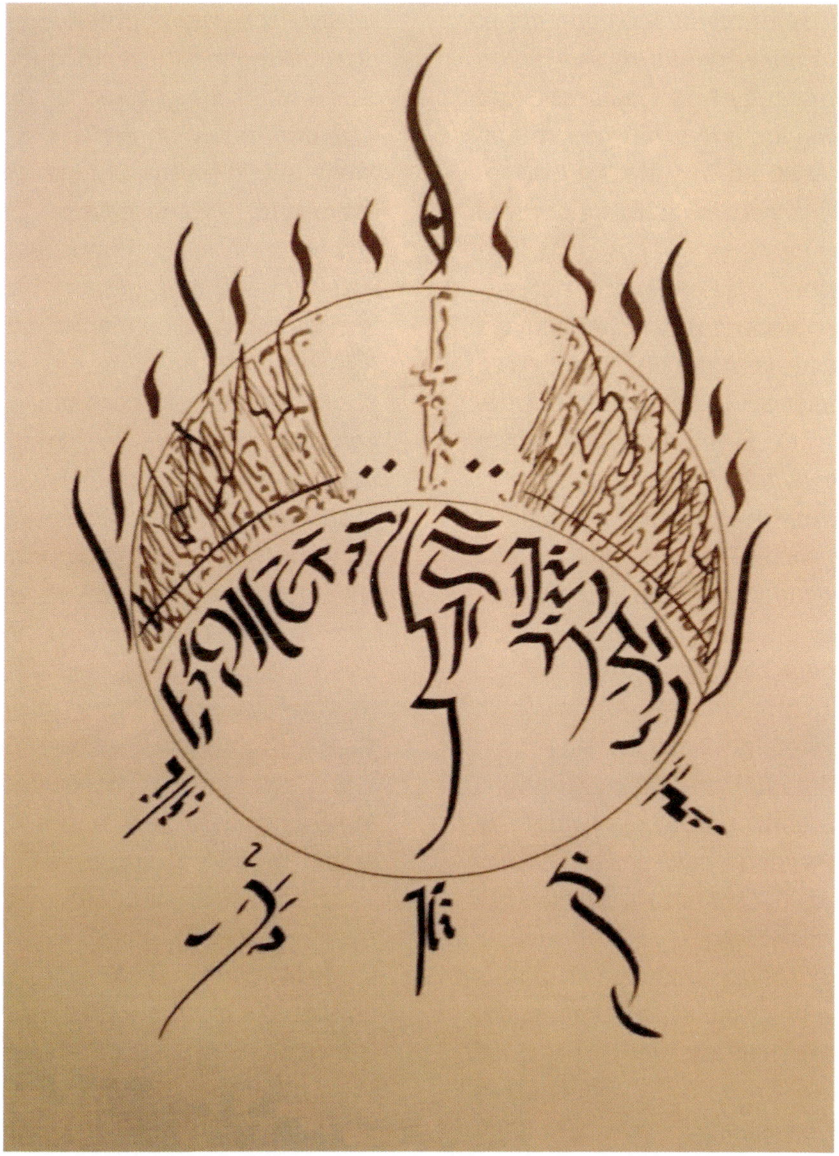

Figure 8 'Creative Spirit', 2022

choke. They vomited, purging the contents of their stomachs into a magically protected vessel (safely disposed of later by a qualified esoteric exorcist). We drive out the mean-spirit of anti-intellectualism and trash culture and replace it with beauty, power, curiosity, and reflective thought!

This, and other magical performances, often with no audience save the Gods, leave faint material traces that can be encountered in various museum collections. In the Renaissance Gallery of the British Museum in London, visitors can see John Dee's shew stone, within which his magical (and wife-swapping) partner Edward Kelley saw angels, and learnt their language. The Museum of Witchcraft & Magic in Cornwall holds on loan the Baphomet mask belonging to the Magical Pact of the Illuminates of Thanateros, British Isles Section. This mask was worn by initiates in rites where, through chanting, drumming and the intoning of barbarous words of power, they would become possessed by that horned spirit. I wore the mask in public myself once while on top of the Fourth Plinth in Trafalgar Square as part of a participatory Arts event. During my allotted hour on the plinth, I summoned Baphomet and invited viewers (the whole thing was broadcast on SkyArts) to donate money to the Witchcraft Museum, which back in 2009 was in dire need of a new roof. The mask had had at least one previous public appearance at the London fetish club Torture Garden during a Black Mass celebrated in honour of Anton Szandor LaVey some years previously. But these public events are exceptions. Magic, in the sense of occultism, tends to be a business that, in contradistinction to the magic of the stage, happens behind closed temple doors, deep in the woods or inside our own imaginations. Its emergence into a public space as ceremonial practice is, in certain respects, uncommon. The same is actually true of artistic practice; for while there is public art and celebrated artists, most art is in fact hidden. Not only as Outsider Art but as the everyday folk art and creative practice in all its forms that never makes it into a museum or gallery, into publication, or the canon of art history.

The other side of the coin is that many individuals who are primarily described as artists profess an active engagement in the occult. To fully understand and appreciate their work, knowing something about magic is essential; how can you comprehend the films of Derek Jarman without knowing about his alchemy of light as an occult practice? Or the shamanic paintings of Jackson Pollock? Let alone those more explicitly esoteric artists such as Remedios Varo or Rosaleen Norton? A few years ago, it would have been anathema in the Euro-American academy to discuss the interplay of magic and art, however thankfully today all that has changed. We are seeing a pronounced academic-artistic-magical revival; it's now okay to talk about occult culture, and even profess to our own practice, at least within some sections of the academy.

In Britain this renewed appreciation of the relationship between magic and art perhaps began to stir with The Dark Monarch show at Tate St Ives in 2009. Since then, changing opinions in academia have been nurtured by many individuals, groups such as the Black Mirror Research Network, and through publications and events such as the Visions of Enchantment conference at the University of Cambridge in 2014.

This change of culture and the re-engagement with the esoteric is in no small part a consequence of practitioner-academics being brave and feeling secure enough to own their position as both bona-fide researchers and as practising occultists. We're now in a period where the relationship between the academy, art and magic is seen as a valid area of enquiry. As an example of this, in October of 2022 the British Art Network hosted a conference about the curation of magical art, magic and esotericism: 'This seminar aims to consider how magic's continued importance as counter-cultural force and epistemological strategy might be reflected in art, art history and curation, exploring how magic and esotericism can shape not only the content of an exhibition but how they might, in turn, inform curatorial practice itself.' How meta is that?

Trans-States, the series of inter-disciplinary conferences held at the University of Northampton since 2016, is another one of the spaces in which academics, occultists and artists come together. It was a great honour to be invited by their curatorial team to display some of my magical art at the 2022 conference, and with that show came an opportunity to write an artist's statement:

'My work is an expression of my magical practice. I am interested in liminal psychological and philosophical spaces where meaning is untethered. What do these symbols mean? Are these signs asemic writing? Are they pregnant with novel ideas? Are they transient scrambled sigilic forms or specific arcane glyphs which, by and large, seems to escape from the conventional iconography of occultism? I am reminded of the way that floating, shifting text can be read in the glowing logs of the fire or the textures of stones. Many of these drawings are based on visions received in entheogenic ceremony. Look at all the little faces in the trees...

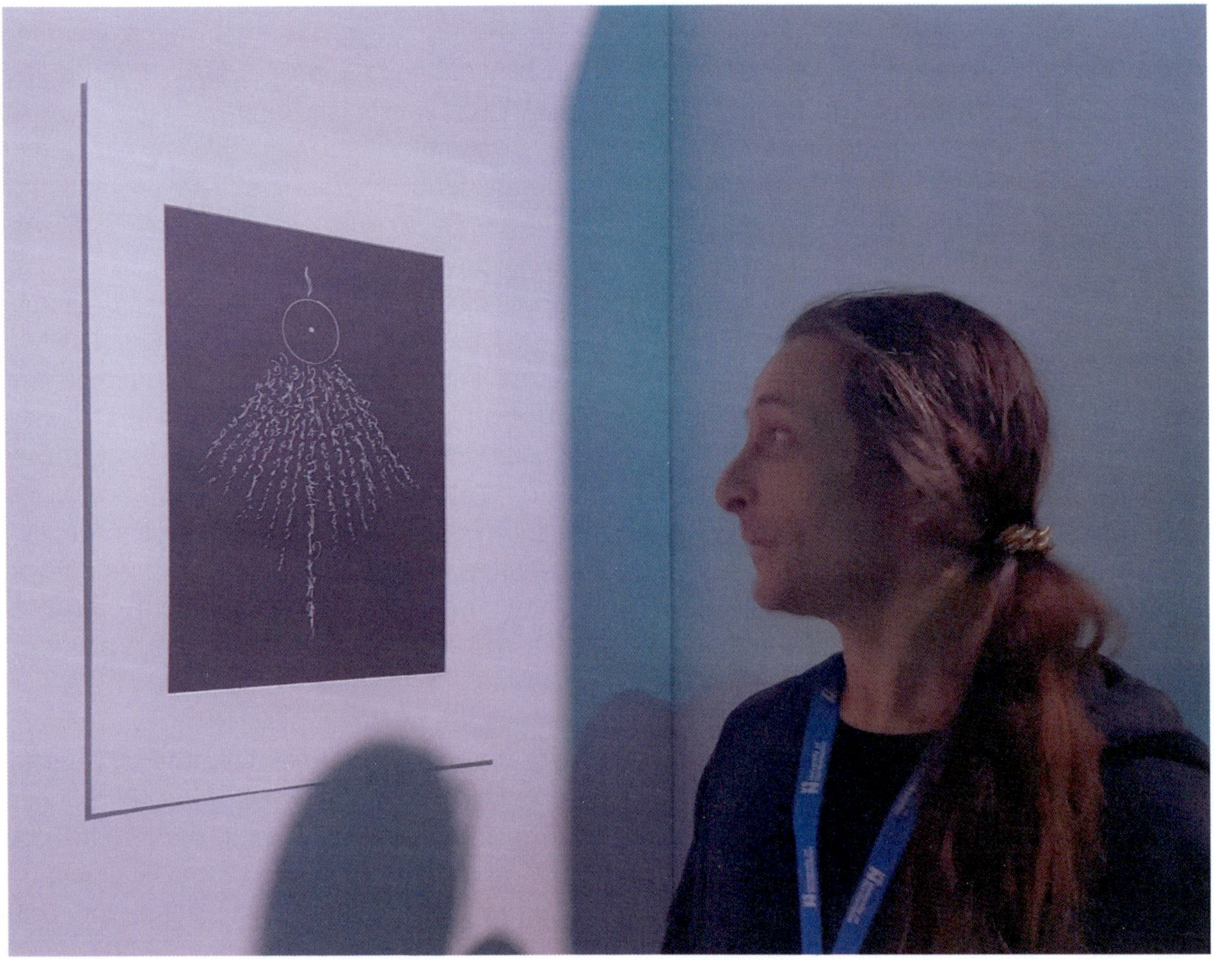

Figure 9 At Trans-States 2022 with my work 'Shamanic Costume', 2022

'*Each work includes an Enchantment associated with the theme of the ritual from which the work arises. An esoteric technology or practice is also provided with each work.*'

That brief and suitably gnomic artist's statement could be unpacked further. A little more of the backstory is in order, to understand where I'm coming from as an artist-occultist.

When I was a child in junior school, at about the age of 10, I encountered the world of calligraphy through one of my teachers who was skilled in that art. Inspired and encouraged (thanks Mr Stacey) I bought pens and ink and experimented with lettering forms, both traditional and innovative. I bought printed copies of catalogues of Letraset and set off exploring the styles of those characters that could be reproduced by hand. Learning to write with a round nib, calligraphy pens, with a brush, and eventually exploring traditional gold illumination on parchment, was a delight, and probably an important corrective to my anxiety about writing (my spelling was poor, with perhaps a suggestion of undiagnosed dyslexia). This early exposure to fancy writing in a variety of styles is at the root of the artwork I produce.

Another important influence on me was the world of Dungeons and Dragons, with a twist. As a child I imbibed the Western magical tradition, its canon of texts, its jargon, and its symbols, filling copious notebooks, from the age of 9 onwards, with Hebrew letters and glyphs of the planets, fixed stars, tables of elemental symbols, esoteric correspondences, and mystical concepts. So, when I encountered D&D In my early teens, I noticed something strange. In both the texts like *The Monster Manual* (Gary Gygax, 1978), and on the miniatures that I purchased from the local Games Workshop, there were symbols that I did not recognise. Signs that pointed towards magic, and yet were not part of the Hermetic Western magical tradition that I was already (by the age of 13) steeped in. What were these mysterious glyphs? What were these curious marks? What did they indicate? What did they mean? Ironically these signs were more occult (hidden) to me than the letters of Theban script, the angelic seals derived from kameas or the glyphs of astrology.

At college, I trained as a graphic designer. I was fascinated by typography and the peculiarities of different fonts, the way that the letter forms themselves communicate information. As a young man I worked in several design studios having trained in what in those days was called DTP (desktop publishing) using early applications such as Adobe PageMaker and CorelDRAW. I created a couple of fonts and put my illustrative and

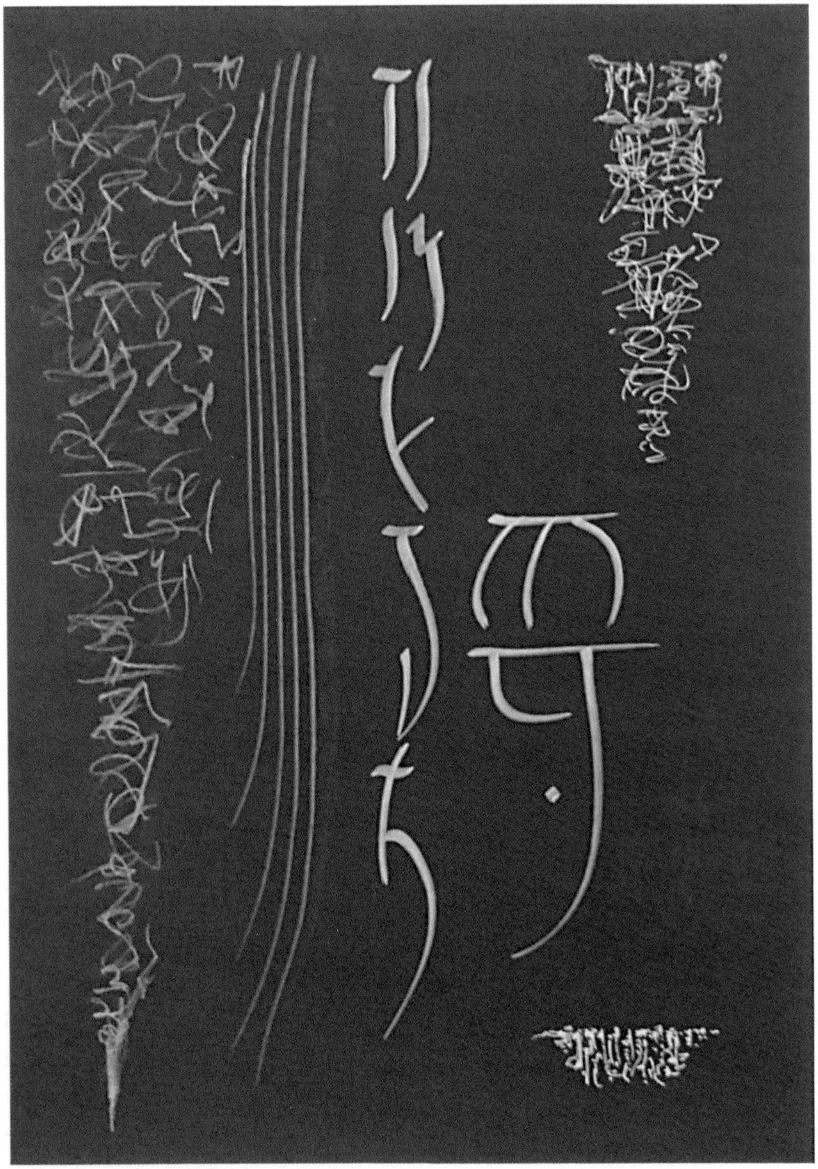

Figure 10 'Descending Siglization', 2022

layout skills to good use designing my self-published 1990s zine *Pagan Voice*. Later I designed flyers for raves in Bristol. As well as working with digital media I kept up my work with physical penmanship; friends would sometimes receive their favourite poem, written in flowing calligraphic script, as a birthday gift.

The deities of writing are typically also the deities of magic. Thoth, ancient Egyptian god of writing and magic presided over a culture where words, especially written words, were pregnant with *Heka*, the ancient Egyptian word for magical power. Hieroglyphic spells were written on papyrus steeped in water or beer so that the intention of those incantations, typically healing, would be transferred into the liquid. Once drunk the spell would go to work. Similar methods are reprised these days by sigil wielding magicians, where rather than discrete letters, the intentions are encoded into unique, often ephemeral monograms or sigils. I recall in one magical group I was part of in Brighton around the millennium how we incised the sigil of Fotamecus, a spirit with the power to alter time itself, into biscuits we baked. The ritual served both to ensoul and to feed the spirit, an entity first contacted by some chaos magicians in the United States:

'Fotamecus was originally a sigil created in spring of 1996 when I was showing the Mad Prophet some sigilization techniques. The Mad Prophet kept the paper used for the demonstration and began using it when he was driving, the sigil's intent being to 'Force Time Into Compression.' Ruben, a friend of both me and the Mad Prophet, was brought in on this, and two people began directing energy at it.

Fotamecus crossed the Sigil/Servitor line after both Ruben and the Mad Prophet attended a Metallica concert in Sacramento at which Quinn is said to have smiled evilly when looking at the crowd and muttered 'Free gnosis...' before opening himself to channel and becoming a one-man-mosh. On the drive back, both Ruben and the Mad Prophet dumped the excess energy into Fotamecus and made it home in half the time it should have taken.'

Fenwick Rysen, 'Fotamecus: Viral Time Compression/Expansion Servitor', chaosmatrix.org, 27th June 1997.

By eating the biscuits we made our own pact with Fotamecus,

'*...to assist us in expanding or contracting our subjective perception of time. I say 'subjective' advisedly—while we live in a world of atomic clocks and the connected pulse of internet timekeeping—as Dr Who* *observes, 'People assume that time is a strict progression of cause to effect, but *actually* from a non-linear, non-subjective viewpoint—it's more like a big ball of wibbly wobbly... timey wimey... stuff.'*

Julian Vayne, The Magical Technology of Fotamecus, TheBlogofBaphomet.com, 10th July 2013

Writing then, of sigils and of characters, is deeply magical stuff. In the beginning was the word but when the word takes form and when form can in term be decoded and arise again as the word, we are in the territory not only of the sacred but of the powerful and the skilful; the world of the magician, the person who aspires to do magic. (The word itself comes from the Proto-Indo-European root 'magh' meaning 'to be able, have power.')

The word as symbol contains mystery which is encountered through the process of decoding. At the time of writing this essay I've been in correspondence with a person commissioned by the Massachusetts Institute of Technology to write about the origins of cryptography, including its relationship with occultism. Seems it's not only the arts academy that are renewing their interest with the esoteric arts. This is a potent magic, the way in which sound becomes form, which in turn becomes sound by decoding if read aloud, or transforms into silent imaginings if read silently inside one's head (a practice surprisingly uncommon until relatively recently).

When the All-Father Odin, the great proto-shaman of the Northern peoples, had spent nine long, hungry days and nights pinned to the world tree Yggdrasil, a sacrifice of himself to himself, with a roar he reached down to the ground. Unlike Buddha who simply touched the earth, Odin snatched up from the material world fragments of the Great Mystery. These fragments he offered to his people as the runes. A row of angular letters, runes are ideal for carving into stone, engraving on iron, and risting across the grain of wood. Further south, other sacred letters curved their way onto pages. Paper, invented in China around the 1st century AD, was brought by Muslim merchants traveling the Silk Road in the 8th century to the Middle East, first as commodity and then as a technique that could be replicated. Carbon and gum Arabic were mixed, and brush strokes forming the names of God curled their way across the page in the fluid cursive scripts of Arabic, Persian and Hebrew. The hotter the country, it would seem, the curlier the writing.

Further east in the homeland of paper, Chinese pictograms had deftly emerged into elegant manifestation as early as the 12th century BCE, including of course characters for the Sun (rì 日) and the Moon (yuè 月). Cangjie, the legendary inventor of Chinese writing, derived his letters by observing the marks left by animals on the sand.

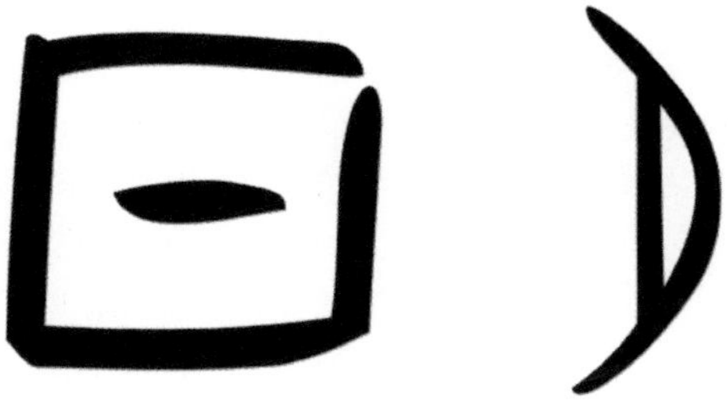

Figure 11 The Sun and the Moon, as written upon oracle bones over 3,000 years ago

Across the great ocean the Mayan civilisation encoded meaning into logogramic shapes that, to my eye, look like diagrams of microscopic cellular structures. Writing does not emerge fully-formed but slowly grows out of more ancient roots, indeed some aspects of the relationship between image and sound are deeply rooted in our human bodies.

The shapes of letters straddle the line between the arbitrary artifacts of culture and the inherent common architecture of human perception. The non-arbitrary mental association between form and some speech sounds is most notable in the bouba/kiki effect first documented in 1929 by psychologist and phenomenologist Wolfgang Köhler. In Köhler's experiment we are introduced to two shapes and asked, which is bouba and which kiki?

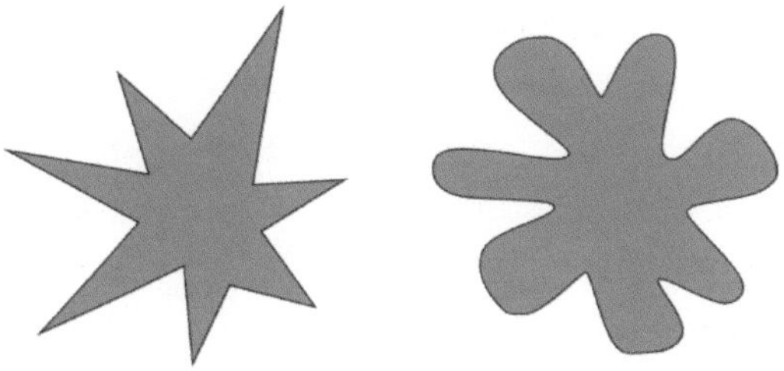

Across language groups and cultures, the vast majority of people will opine that bouba is the shape on the right, while kiki is on the left. The spiky sound of 'k' is even echoed in the Latin letter form whereas the 'b' of bouba is a rounded character. Similar, though somewhat less consistently, sound and shape associations exist and seem to be rooted in human physiology. The hissing of a serpent, for example, is often represented by the same shape as the undulating ophidian itself. In Latin characters we have 's'. However, the method of writing is also a factor as it is with the incised cuneiform characters, the stark runes or the curvaceous calligraphy of Malayalam. Passing through the physical requirements of drawing a metallic nib evenly across parchment, the

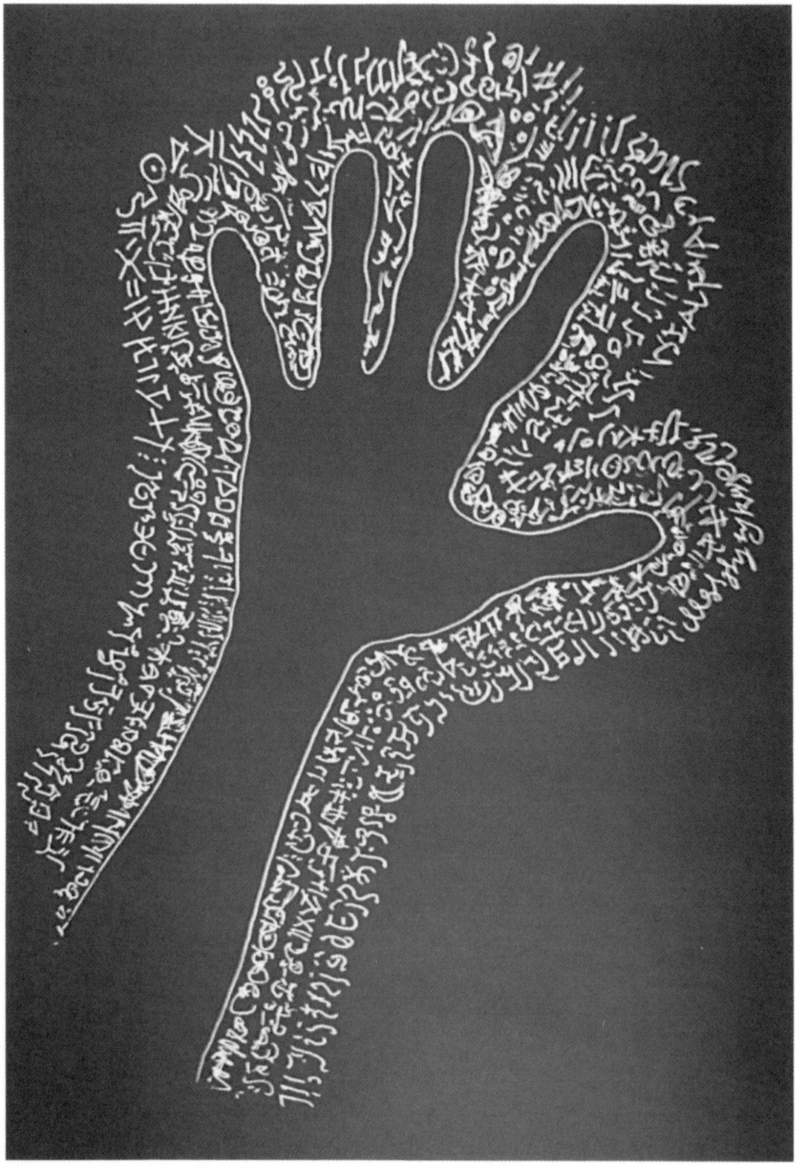

Figure 12 'Hand Illuminated', 2022

sibilant, sinuous 's' mutates into the angular strokes of the Gothic blackletter script.

As well as the early influence of calligraphic writing and my fascination with fonts, years later I would encounter strangely morphing symbols, pregnant with meaning and yet enticingly undecodable, in the heart of the psychedelic experience. I remember seeing these symbols at a peyote circle more than a quarter of a century ago. For that first ritual we used *Psilocybe semilanceata*, rather than the peyote cactus itself, though the ceremonial design and lineage of its facilitators was that of the Native American Church. I watched the flames as the Fire Keeper raked glowing the coals, held in the arms of the crescent moon altar, into wide incandescent shapes; a thunderbird, a radiant sun, a heart. I saw the flames burning the sticks of the arrow fire and how, in my psychedelically enhanced vision, there was writing there. Glowing and moving, transient, mysterious letters written out in a morphing, shifting alien and yet somehow distinctly recognisable language. Years later I remember smoking N,N-DMT beside the Atlantic Ocean, looking at the great slabs of cliff descending to the beach, and the sharp broken teeth of black sedimentary rocks marching into the surf. On these surfaces there were changes of light and shade; the colours of the geology beneath a veneer of lichen and mosses, moving and shifting like the innumerable layers of some peculiar organic Photoshop. Every surface was covered with thousands of intricate characters, with writing—curved loops like Arabic calligraphy and rune-like angular marks.

The work that I produce grows from this world of strange graphic images and mysterious letters encountered in altered states of consciousness. In the art I produce I'm more interested in hinting at meaning, at suggesting interpretation than making it explicit. I occasionally include clearly esoteric glyphs and forms in my art to help orientate the viewer and practitioner. I say 'practitioner' because I hope that people who buy these works will use them in their own Great Work. Each work is a spirit, a magical being, a portal. For that reason, I only sell original artworks. I'm not interested in factory production of art any more than I would enjoy the factory production of ceremony.

The practice into which the owner or viewer is invited to step, is the operation of attempting to decode the glyphs; or perhaps going beyond that game, and learning how to sit with Mystery, looking and listening to the lack of a definitive meaning and what that cesura conjures for each of us. This, for me, is the heart of the magical process. Magic, whatever its claims to control or influence the world, is fundamentally about following the ever-receding Mystery of the universe. While esoteric approaches such as chaos magic have emphasized the importance of verifiable results, I believe that the meaning of magic is much deeper than that which can be understood by simple causal thinking. Magic is a polyvocal, multi-levelled, complex weaving of the web of Wyrd which points towards the interplay of curiosity, awareness, interpretation, and meaning, ever following the unknown in the world.

This, for me, is the art of magic and the magic of art.

---

[i] Fluxus: Art movement of the 1960s which professed disdain for the formally defined world of art (museums, galleries), the limitation of art to professional artists. Promoted the idea of art as open to all, and creativity as a project that everyone should engage with all the time.

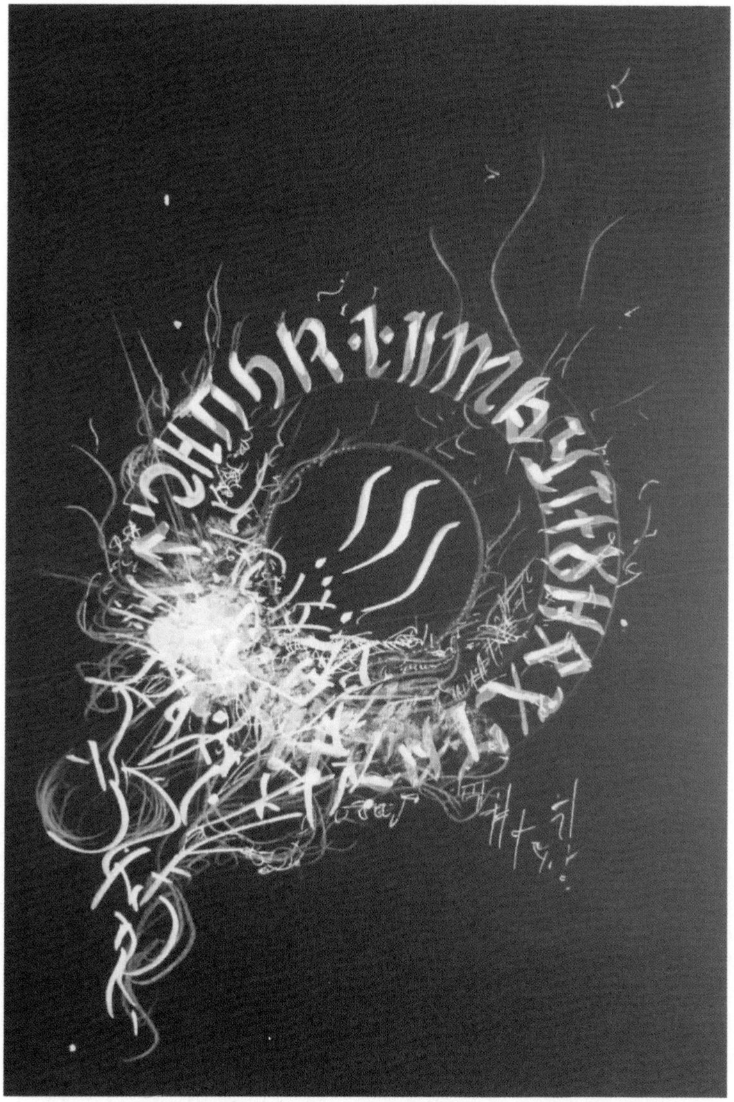

Figure 13 'The Detonation of Language', 2022

There's a witch in place mutating

Kate Southworth

Hoping for spiritual visions I spend much of my childhood slipping into daydreams and painting. Illness and its concomitant stillness nurture a contemplative aspect within my somewhat restricted life. I draw. I paint. I find. I develop, or perhaps hold onto, a capacity to move easily into unconscious worlds, and to sense the enormity of the cosmos that surrounds me. I experience a kind of telepathic link to strangers, animals and plants; feel their distress and their joy. Discussions about socialism and equality provide balance. I begin to think about how to account for my experiences of the world, and why the categories available to me seem not to fit. I think the rational segregation of life devalues who I am and I set out to find the missing fragments. At the age of 16 I begin to study painting, become politically active and, in a haphazard way, continue to explore and encounter the rich other worlds beyond the mundane. Seemingly isolated threads of magic, rituals, spells, yoga, esotericism, psychoanalysis, dialectical materialism, distributed networks, spirituality, alchemy come into my life and little by little I see that they are connected together through loops and holes; crochet-like. Thus begins my alchemical life; the transformational dance between mercury and moon and sun. Luna and Sol approach with double-headed roses proffered the left-handed way. The dove's rosary makes six. Blooms brush your chin and through heavy garments I feel your touch. We meet.

I think the soul paints itself transforming. I think, perhaps, there's a witch in place mutating. Mostly, I struggle to perceive it; an almost-thing around which I unknowingly circumambulate. The nearness of it brings unusual contentment yet, unfamiliar with the terrain I wander away lost. I plod on. Never really abandoning the mystic ways prompts patterns of devoted discovery. Indigo swoops its magic and that longed-for linking returns. It calls me home. The painting really begins with the emergence of the Prima Materia; an encounter that is not guaranteed, even though desired. Its bright blackness pulsates intensities that vibrate to my soul. If I project my unconscious web into matter, I also take time to sit with what manifests. Sometimes, I brush away unfamiliar fragments too quickly; missing their touch. They return. Sometimes,

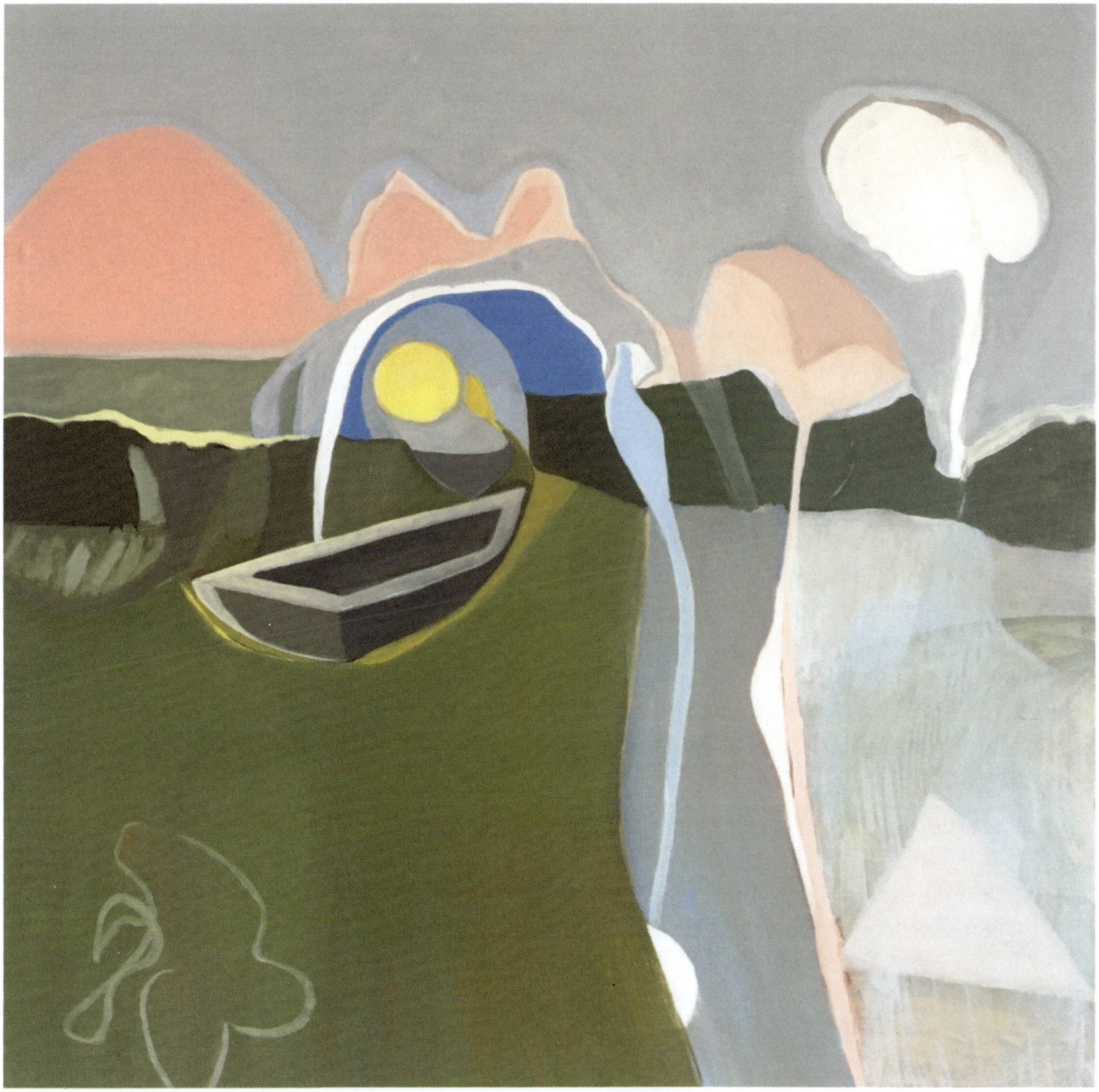

Figure 14 'The Moon and The Sun', 2023. Oil on Canvas 50 cm x 50 cm.

with Luna's aid, I feel them; recognise them without consciously knowing them, and listen in stillness. I sit with my work as if with a stranger, hearing it. It happens quietly; slipping along a border between invisible filament and rounded shape and it grows. Then on that loud stormy night I wake thinking myself dead. I dream abject emptiness until I hear them breathing alongside me. Hovering between almost unbearable intimacy and almost aloneness, telepathic moments seep into being and the traces paint my micro-decisions with something more.

I see new forms emerge from the colours, lines, shapes. They seem to fade into different psychic registers, organs, energies, senses; each vibrating a different tone, speaking a different language. With Sol's aid I learn not to dismiss their awkwardness too readily; and to question whose version of painting I'm inhabiting. I become a little more aware of how my body moves, how I feel, what I hear, as the brush touches the canvas. If I attempt to fit the contents to a pre-existing schema, it seems to fall apart. I continue, for a while, in the tight enclosure of the paintings until I feel invisible filaments linking me outwards. This brings relief and I begin to spin my threads towards it. A magic bead placed in the pocket, a joint awakening, differentiated for each, spell enacted. Through symbols, maps and diagrams I paint the strands to other psyches in the landscape: the veiled boat moored halfway up a hill describes something real, and as I sit in silence with the painting, I seem to hear its story. The mutating witch feels brought to birth with cosmic spirit in the blackness teeming with life. A canvas, left-handedly knotted with uneven threads, sits in a cloud of vermillion. Its divine blackness embeds circles into three-dimensional space. Two strands loop wildly east to west, each with an almost twist, perhaps of infinity. The square holds itself cheerfully as something resolved-enough, and its joyful imperfections radiate life.

Alchemy begins with the emergence of the First Matter (Prima Materia) and ends with the creation of the Philosophers' Stone (Lapis Philosophorum). The stone; a powder, a tincture, perhaps the Prima Materia itself, is, amongst other things, referred to as Lapis Occultus and Arcanum (mystery, deep secret, elixir, secret remedy). Once manifested, the ripened stone then transforms through four seasons; participating in calendrical processes and relations of gestation, birth, growth, blossoming, fading, dying, absence, emptiness, and birth again. Sometimes alchemy appears to be paradoxical, sometimes nonsensical. It slides between layers of meaning in a single breath. What begins as something spiritual twists into magical, psychological, artistic, ethical, political, and technological and back again. This multi-dimensional orientation allows for all possibilities within and between its borders. Without borders alchemy falls into chaos, and it most surely isn't chaos. Its organisational form, porous and shifting, manifests transformation; including its own transformation.

The Prima Materia, perhaps the most mysterious, complex concept in alchemy, has been described variously as sun, moon, sea, salt, love, consciousness, soul, dew, blood, urine, dirt, placenta, and hundreds more concepts. Carl Jung described the Prima Materia as a projection of the unconscious, and in particular that aspect of the unconscious that he refers to as the Objective Psyche. He agreed with the alchemists that 'when the idea of the Prima Materia is understood, the problem of alchemy is already half-solved, its questions half-answered'[i]. The Objective Psyche for Jung is part of the deepest layer of the unconscious; an archaic, instinctual realm shared by all humans. If the Prima Materia is a projection of the objective psyche, then the Philosophers' Stone (Lapis Philosophorum), is a projection of the Self; a powerful energy, which guides our perpetual unfolding towards becoming who we really are. It connects us to our being which includes the spiritual, the numinous, the transcendent. The Self is the source of the drive to individuate, to bring the conscious and the unconscious into optimal balance. In alchemy, the soul builds the bridge between the spirit and the body. The unfiltered psychic experience of the objective psyche manifests itself as Archetypes; forms, patterns, elements which find expression in dreams, myths, fairy tales, religion, and some forms of art.

For the alchemists the distinction between subject and object remained blurred, and the boundary between one and the other porous. Inner psychic states were projected outwards onto the material being examined, and qualities found in the material itself were regarded as part of alchemist's inner world. The alchemists recorded in writings and drawings the results of their experiments with matter without codifying or interpreting them. As such—and in contrast to archetypal images contained within religious traditions—they describe raw and immediate experiences of the unconscious. Contemporaneous and subsequent analyses of alchemists' findings involve the introduction of conceptual frameworks, filters, through which to analyse the material.

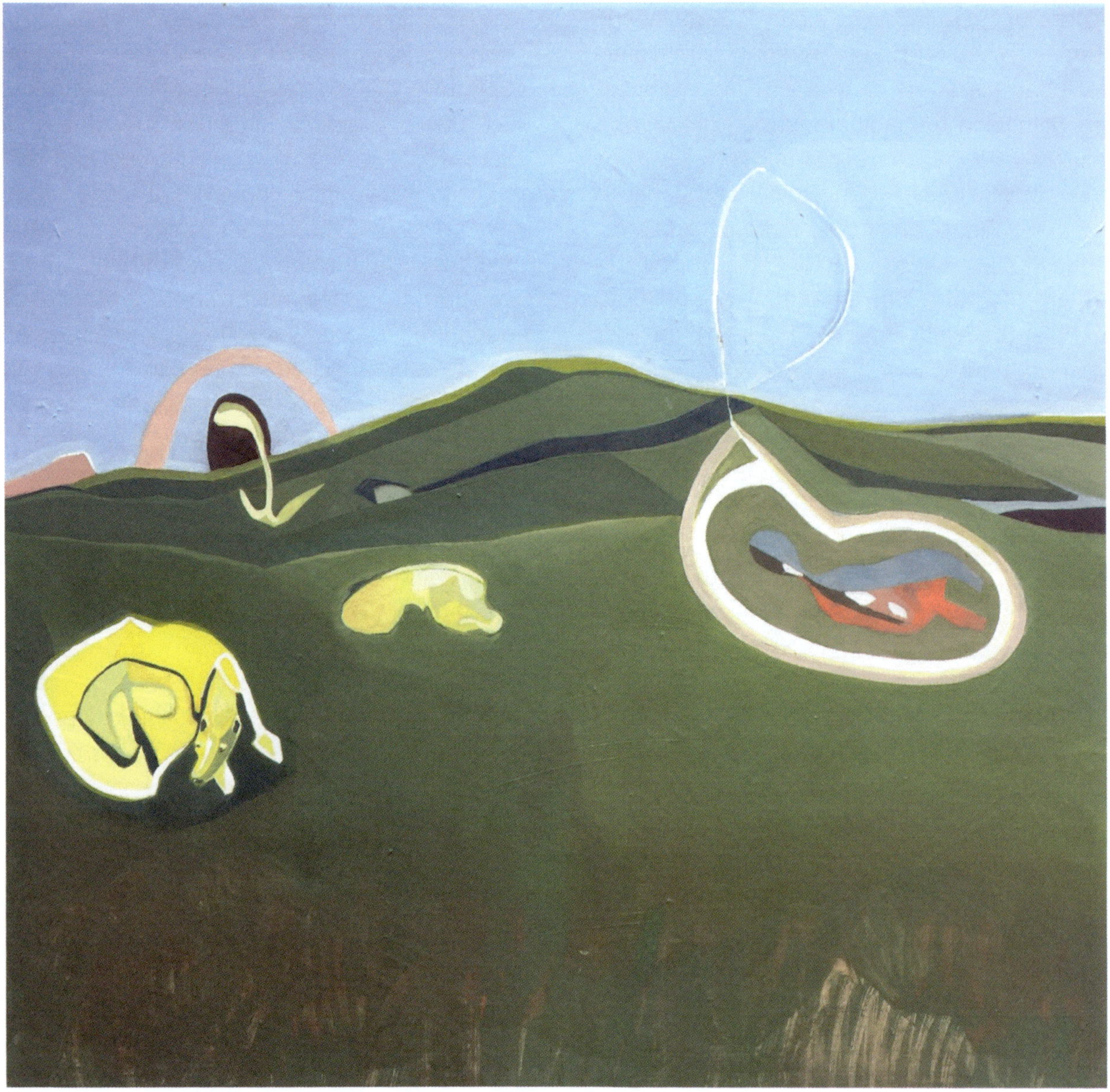

Figure 15 'Cosmic Landscape', 2003. Oil on Canvas, 80cm x 80cm.

Jung's conceptual framework included, amongst other things, the belief that parts of the psyche function outside of rational notions of time and space and that to account for the world in its entirety would require the conceptualisation of another dimension. He believed that the archetypes and figures within the objective psyche were a living reality, not restricted to the individual psyche, and in some way connected to a cosmic order[ii].

Analysis of raw alchemic writings and drawings, then, encourages thinking about the ontological features of psyche; the range of processes and relations with which humans abstract 'elements' with which to think the world. If such elements pre-exist within the psyche and within the cosmos, it doesn't necessarily follow that humans have evolved the capacity to fully perceive them. If they are devised by humans, upon what values are they based? These elements connect to the ways in which we paint, think, imagine, dream, define, remember, and reason.[iii] For psychoanalyst, Jacques Lacan, the elements with which we think the world are inscribed in language, and through a child's acquisition of language, a particular way of thinking the world and a particular way of being in the world is also acquired. This, he terms the Symbolic register, and it resides within the unconscious.

For German media theorist Friedrich Kittler, the Symbolic is not only inscribed in language, but also in technology. For Kittler, media determine our situation; they inscribe upon us their logic, their ways of working, and we think the world through their filter. The Romantic poets and novelists managed to weave the spiritual, the bodily, and the emotional into the symbolic of the written word through which these non-rational qualities were ascribed value and meaning. Disrupted by the new technologies of the early 20th century the Symbolic begins to look inwards towards its own functions and operations; restricting its sphere to the laws of abstraction themselves. Here, the spiritual, emotional, and corporeal are denied entry into the Symbolic, and packed off into separate spheres—what Lacan, followed by Kittler, refers to as the psychic registers of the Imaginary and the Real. The Imaginary tunes desire but is shaped by the Symbolic. The Real works in tension with the Symbolic and the Imaginary: It is impossible to express in language and is inaccessible to the Symbolic. However, the Real does not disappear, that which is unspeakable or unrepresentable will always return in the Real.

As the century advances, the passageway to meaning constricts, and the correlation of the Symbolic with the computational intensifies. With the new digital and networked technologies, the language of the Symbolic speaks only rules, protocols, instructions, formulae; the last vestiges of the numinous, transcendent, spiritual aspects of psyche obliterated. Yet Magic doesn't disappear, it returns again in the Real. Distributed networks, such as the internet and blockchain, replace centralised, hierarchical structures with distributed, flattened networks. Steeped in contradiction, they facilitate open, democratic, participative and collaborative processes and practices, yet at the same time operate by means of their specific operational force: protocol. This Network Symbolic becomes entirely unable to relate directly to the human. It re-categorises human subjectivity, activity and agency to 'content', incapable of affecting the system, and upon which the logic of the system is inscribed. It incorporates and assimilates into its logic all the systems, conceptual frameworks, logics, that facilitate human and machinic exchange. Now, we must challenge the very logic of the Network Symbolic as the only passage to meaning.

Artist and psychoanalyst, Bracha Ettinger, suggests that the Symbolic order, which informs much Western thought, does so under claims of neutrality and universality and she names it *phallic*: not as masculine, but as that which is premised on the oppositions, absence/presence, on/off, plus/minus. She conceptualises and theorises an expansion of the Lacanian Symbolic to accommodate the possibility of several supplementary signifiers that challenge the Phallus as the one and only sovereign signifier ruling the Symbolic[iv]. The Phallic Symbolic has been challenged politically by Karl Marx and Friedrich Engels through their work on the dialectical method through which, I suggest, they posit a rational *and* non-Phallic mode of abstracting elements with which to think the world.

Ettinger's proposal of a supplementary space, the Matrix, within the Symbolic does not displace Phallic logic. It adds to the understanding of the psyche and radically expands 'the range of processes and dimensions that constitute human subjectivity' and the passage to meaning.[202] Arising in the Real of the late stages of pregnancy, the archaic zone of pre-natal/pre-maternal human-becoming posits an archaic subjectivizing encounter that generates as its core elements a primordial severality defined by a shared borderspace and the operations of borderlinking. As a symbol, like the Phallus, the Matrix is not about literal or physiological organs. It captures the proto-psychic potentiality (for the becoming infant) and the traumatic psychic event (for the becoming mother) that shape the post-natal trauma/jouissance and the later phantasies and ultimately conceptualization of *non-phallic relations between subjective entities*. She proposes the concept of Metramorphosis as the means by which the elements that are excluded from and by the Symbolic order can be registered. A Matrixial Symbolic sphere allows for *more than one* signifier ruling the Symbolic.

Following Ettinger then, resistance to the intensification of rationalised, instrumentalised, commodified relations within the everyday, comes not with rejecting the system, for that falls prey to its defining Phallic logic; but through sub-symbolising supplementary spaces. Perhaps we can re-imagine the alchemical operation *Separatio*—Separation of the Elements—within reference to Matrixial pre-organisational form. It would involve questioning the frameworks with which we view the world. We might ask: where and how we draw boundaries, where and how we decide where one thing begins and another thing ends, what emerges at the boundaries between one thing and another, whether the boundaries are mutable. The process of abstracting and almost-abstracting elements not only produces symbols and sub-symbols, it contributes to the fabric of the Symbolic itself.

I look to other artists who embrace this Matrixial ontology by weaving the spiritual, numinous and transcendent with the rational. Although the grid is usually associated with abstract and mathematical thinking and seen as being reflective of the logical order of the mind, the slight irregularities in Agnes Martin's hand-drawn grids quietly destabilises its logic. Martin makes a place in which subtle feelings emerge in non-hierarchical relation to the grid, such that neither one nor the other dominates or incorporates the other. Lawrence Alloway sees the seamless surface of Martin's grids signifying 'for all its linear precision, an image dissolving': something 'half-way between a rectangular system of coordinates and a veil'.[v] Although it is the *materiality* of the grid that interests us today, Rosalind Krauss suggests that when Mondrian and Malevich paint grids they 'are not discussing canvas or pigment or graphite or any other form of matter. They are talking about Being or Mind or Spirit. From their point of view, the grid is a staircase to the Universal, and they are not interested in what happens below the concrete'.[vi] Transcendental forces and spirituality inform the series of systematic grid-based drawings created by Swiss artist, scientist and healer, Emma Kunz. Hilma af Klint's paintings sometimes resemble diagrams and formulae, referencing complex spiritual ideas.

In my paintings and in other elements, womb-like shapes connect with cosmic landscapes, reflecting transformations of the calendar year, pregnancy, birth and the maternal, and the co-emergence of life. Birds, horses, serpents, seahorses, and strange, otherworldly creatures seem to fade into worlds beyond our own. Sometimes, web-like filaments hover around these symbols; liminal and interstitial spaces between psyche and landscape, self and other, human and non-human, material and spiritual. The paintings, following the alchemists, begin as unconscious projections onto the matter. Through gentle reflective processes some elements are brought to a state that hovers between unconscious and conscious awareness. As aspects become more conscious, I take those revelations into the spells and rituals. Their instructional form is particularly interesting to me and offers a way to work directly with the protocological in a fragilizing and transformative way.

I think of my artworks as nets of elements and partial elements; paintings, magic, alchemy, writing, rituals, recipes, fragile protocols, gardening, spells, shadow concepts, lists of instability. The elements do not necessarily exist in the same place or time as each other. Sometimes elements remain invisible and unheard; undocumented. Some lie dormant for years until called into (re)being. Sometimes, they emerge spontaneously and sometimes, they co-emerge telepathically. The elements are organised in non-hierarchical, non-centralised, non-linear relations with each other. I visualise these elements as interconnecting webs of knots and holes in diverse yarns. The fragile net form of my work both participates in, and attempts to resist, the distributed network form by adopting a Matrixial strategy of *and* and *and*; protocol and fragilization; symbols and sub-symbols; geometry and healing.

---

[i] Carl Jung, Lecture XI, 11th July 1941

[ii] Carl Jung, Memories, Dreams, Reflections, 335–336.

[iii] Bertell Ollman, Dance of the Dialectic, 61.

[iv] See for example: Bracha Lichtenberg Ettinger. *Matrix-Borderlines*. Oxford: Museum of Modern Art, 1993. Bracha Lichtenberg Ettinger. 'Copoiesis'. *Ephemera: Theory and Politics in Organization* 5, X (2005): 703–713, accessed June 6, 2009, www.ephemeraweb.org/journal/5- X/5-Xettinger.pdf.

[v] Lawrence Alloway, *Agnes Martin,* cited in Strickland, *Minimalism: Origins,* 94.

[vi] Rosalind Krauss, 'Grids'. Originality of the Avant-garde and Other Modernist Myths, 181.

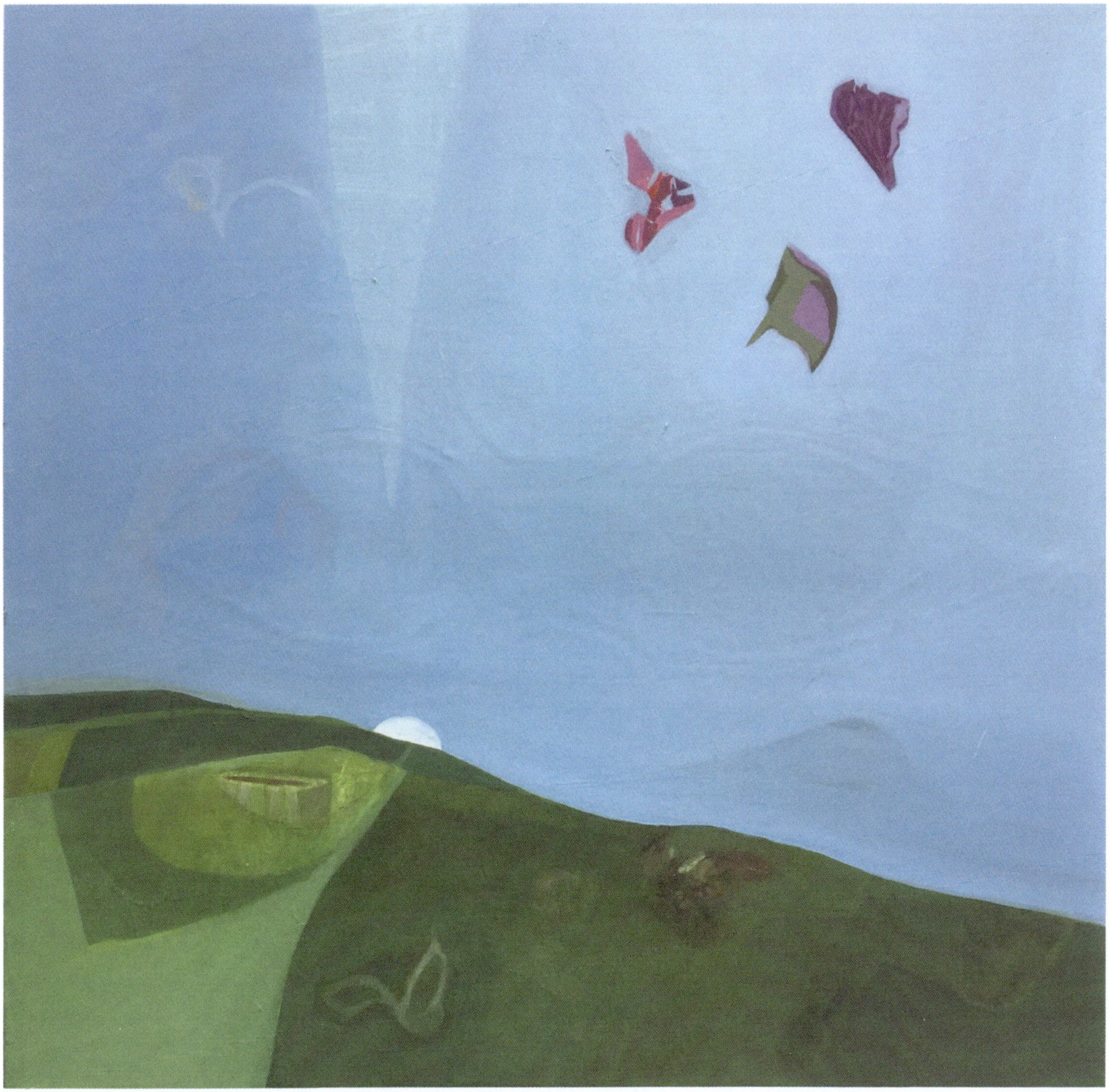

Figure 16 'Sharing a Symbolic Life', 2023. Oil on Canvas 70cm x 70cm.

Artists' information

Greg Humphries:
http://greghumphriesart.co.uk/

Julian Vayne:
https://julianvayne.com/

Kate Southworth:
https://www.katesouthworth.art/

Printed in Great Britain
by Amazon

30439162R00039